The BIBLE& Science

Wayne Jackson

Courier Publications
Stockton, CA

The Bible and Science

©2000 by Courier Publications

ISBN 0-9678044-2-6
$9.95

Additional copies may be ordered from:

Courier Publications
P.O. Box 55265
Stockton, CA 95205

http://www.christiancourier.com

DEDICATION

This volume is gratefully dedicated to the generous Christian men and women who have supported our teaching of biblical truth on the world wide web — http://www.christiancourier.com.

We are truly laborers together in the Lord.

TABLE OF CONTENTS

PREFACE   1

CHAPTER 1
SCIENCE IS NOT A SACRED COW   3

CHAPTER 2
IS THE BIBLE SCIENTIFICALLY CREDIBLE?   13

CHAPTER 3
THE BIBLE AND ASTRONOMY   21

CHAPTER 4
THE BIBLE AND OCEANOGRAPHY   31

CHAPTER 5
THE BIBLE AND GEOLOGY   43

CHAPTER 6
THE BIBLE AND BIOLOGY   55

CHAPTER 7
THE BIBLE AND ANTHROPOLOGY   67

CHAPTER 8
THE BIBLE AND ANATOMY-PHYSIOLOGY   79

CHAPTER 9
THE AMAZING HUMAN MIND   91

CHAPTER 10
THE BIBLE AND MODERN PSYCHOLOGY   103

CHAPTER 11
ARE SCIENCE AND FAITH COMPATIBLE?   117

CHAPTER 12
THE BIBLE AND ARCHAEOLOGY   131

CHAPTER 13
THE BIBLE, GEOGRAPHY,
AND ANCIENT CULTURE   145

PREFACE

It is an exciting time to be alive. Space travel, instant, worldwide communication via the internet, and laser surgery — the technology boggles the mind. But have we outgrown that ancient and revered Book which our ancestors held so dear? Has modern science made the Scriptures obsolete? The fact of the matter is, true science, and a correct view of the Bible, are in perfect harmony. And both are important to our lives.

If God exists (the evidence is overwhelming that He does), and if He is the ultimate Author of the Bible (there is powerful proof that He is), then we have every right to expect that the Scriptures will be perpetually relevant for mankind. One simply cannot "outgrow" the Mind of the everlasting God!

May one assert that the "spiritual" truths of the Bible are meaningful, but its "scientific" references are flawed? No, that is not consistent. The "sum" of the various parts of sacred Writ are "truth" (Psa. 119:160 ASV). The Scriptures are scientifically credible. In fact, "science" never quite "catches up" with Scripture.

In a time of much religious and moral confusion, the author sends forth this volume, hoping that it will help sincere souls who desire to know the true character of God's Word in a world of increasing complexity.

Much gratitude is extended to my son, Jared, for his technical assistance in the production of this book, and to my friend, John Board, for his help in "proofing" the manuscript.

CHAPTER 1

SCIENCE IS NOT A SACRED COW

"Science!" Oh, the magic in that word — at least for a lot of folks. For many people, science has become a religion. The laboratory is the "holy place," and the scientist, adorned in his white lab coat, is the "high priest." In fact, many have become so enchanted with science they think they have outgrown the need for God. One writer declares: "The discoveries of astronomers, geologists, and space explorers have undermined the faith of all but the most devout . . . and [even] among believers, God is more likely to be seen as a force or spirit than as an all-seeing watcher over human behavior" (Packard, 27). Richard Dawkins, a professor at Oxford University, says that with the advent of Darwin's theory of evolution, "it [is] possible to be an intellectually fulfilled atheist" (6).

This attitude, though, results from a serious misunderstanding of what science is, and what it can and cannot do.

Science Defined

Exactly what is "science"? The word derives from a Latin term, *scientia,* which simply means "knowledge." One source defines science as: "Knowledge based upon the observation and testing of facts worked into an ordered system acting as a base for new knowledge and a guide for ways of getting it" (Graham, 404). A more simple definition is this: "A branch of study concerned with observation and classification of facts and especially with the establishment of verifiable general laws" (Webster). But as we shall presently see, the word "science" can be used in a rather loose way.

Science Classified

For the purposes of this study, we will classify science under three categories. (1) Physical science deals with non-living materials. For example, astronomy (a study of the stars and other heavenly bodies) and geology (a study of the earth's structure and history) are physical sciences. (2) Biological science deals with living organisms. Zoology (the general study of animals) is a life-science. Physiology (a study of the processes within living things) and anatomy (the study of the structure of living things) are also life-sciences. (3) Then there is an area that may, for lack of a better term, be designated as intellectual science. For example, mathematics is said to be the "science" of the relationship between numbers. Logic is the "science" of correct thinking. It should be noted that not all that is classified as "science" can be investigated in the same way.

The Scientific Method

In coming to a correct view of science, it is extremely important that one have a proper understanding of what is known as "the scientific method." Simply stated, the scientific method is a collection of rules or principles by which one arrives at true "scientific" knowledge. Here are the steps.

First, there is the *observation of facts*. One must be able to perceive the data empirically, i.e., with the senses. If the subject is incapable of sense perception — seeing, hearing, touching, smelling, tasting — it cannot be subjected to the scientific method, hence, according to the definition provided above, could never meet the criterion of true science. Can one "scientifically" prove the existence of God, angels, or the soul? No; these are not subject to the scientific method. It is the case, however, that one can argue the existence of God on logical premises. For a consideration of this, see our book, *Fortify Your Faith*.

Second, there is the *statement of a problem*. Is there a proposition that may account for the facts of a phenomenon? If so, one may propose an hypothesis as a possible explanation. For example, suppose a native from the equatorial region should visit Wyoming. Knowing nothing of the climatic conditions that are characteristic of the northern hemisphere, he observes a pool of water in the evening. The following morning he notes that it has turned to ice. He may wonder: "Did the darkness of night cause the transformation? Did some substance enter the water to produce the change?" He may advance an hypothesis, but whatever his "guess," it will require further investigation.

Third, as suggested by the illustration just given, an hypothesis is subjected to a *testing* process. The testing (experimentation) may subsequently suggest that the hypothesis is either false or perhaps true. Years ago astronomers speculated that there was intelligent life on Mars, because it was believed that "canals," visible through the telescope, were evidence of rational habitation. Subsequent exploration, however, proved that "hypothesis" to be faulty. There is an old saying: "Science without experience is sheer speculation."

Fourth, if an increasing body of experimental evidence seems to support an hypothesis, it may become classified as a *theory*. A theory is not "proof" of anything; it merely suggests that sufficient evidence has been gathered already to warrant further testing.

At this point we must emphasize that any view which cannot be subjected to a testing process, cannot qualify — either as an hypothesis or a theory. Ideas which deal with the origin of the universe, or the origin of human beings, cannot be labeled properly as "science." They are not capable of being tested. This is why some honest scientists are forced to admit that the idea of human evolution does not pass the criterion of a "credible theory" (Danson, 35).

Finally, once a theory is formulated, and then widely tested, the facts may appear to be so firmly established that the phenomenon receives the status of a *law*. It is thus proper to speak of the "laws of reflection" or the "laws of thermodynamics." It is not proper to regard the idea of evolution as a "law," or, indeed, as we pointed out just above, even a "theory."

That is why it was so silly to say, as one document (signed by 177 biologists) asserted a few years back, that evolution is a scientific law "as firmly established even as the rotundity of the earth" (quoted by Bales, 7). That is absurd! Photographs of the earth, made from the moon, document the shape of the earth. Where is objective evidence of Darwinian evolution?

More recently Stephen J. Gould of Harvard asserted that "evolution [is as] well documented as any phenomenon in science, as strongly as the earth's revolution around the sun" (59). His statement is equally extravagant.

The Limitations of Science

Science, then, by its very methodology, is strictly limited in a number of ways.

First, as noted already, science is limited to *sense perception*. If a proposition cannot be physically examined and subjected to empirical analyses, it simply does not fall within the domain of science. Note again the definitions of science that we gave at the beginning of this chapter. A concept may be perfectly valid, such as the idea that God exists. The case for God's existence may be argued quite logically, but it cannot be *demonstrated scientifically*. Jehovah cannot be put into a test tube or placed under a microscope.

The common view regarding the beginning of the universe is called the "Big Bang" theory (though note our qualification of "theory" above). But this notion about the origin of the universe cannot be classified legitimately as "scientific." No historian was there to witness the commencement of the universe; no one captured the event on video. The Big Bang idea is pure speculation — and speculation, in fact, that runs counter to a significant amount of evidence.

Second, science deals with the *present*. Since genuine science demands experimentation, and since experimentation has to occur in the here-and-now, it should be obvious that any event, alleged to have occurred in the ancient past, does not fall within the scope of true science. Again, this rules out the idea of man's supposed evolutionary origin.

Third, science is limited to explaining *how* things work; it cannot address such issues as *why* they happen. Forensic science, for instance, can explain how a bullet is fired from a gun and enters a victim's body, but it cannot determine whether the shooting was a murder or a tragic accident. Other information would be required for that conclusion.

Fourth, science deals only with *matter*, i.e., the material — that which occupies space. In his book, *The Limitations of Science,* J.W.N. Sullivan, described by *Time* magazine as one of the world's "most brilliant interpreters of physics," adamantly stated that "science is confined to a knowledge of structure" (142).

One cannot, for example, scientifically demonstrate the existence of the soul. Attempts to weigh an individual, before and after death, and to determine the density of the human spirit, have been exercises in futility. The case for the human soul must be argued in some fashion other than by the application of scientific rules. Science can neither affirm it nor deny it.

Dr. Louis T. More, who was not sympathetic to Christianity, nonetheless acknowledged: "Science does not embrace all phenomena and it has not, for its use, all the criteria of truth" (354). Again note this from Sullivan: "[S]cience deals with but a partial aspect of reality, and . . . there is [not the] faintest reason for supposing that everything science ignores is less real than the world it accepts" (147).

Fifth, science deals with phenomena that are *repeatable*; it cannot address *unique* events (such as the claim of historical miracles). One evolutionist notes that in science, "observations and experiments must always be reported in such a way that they can be repeated and verified, and must *always be repeated and verified before they are incorporated into the body of knowledge*" (Curtis, 12; emp. WJ).

Did life accidentally jump-start itself several billion years ago? Evolutionists claim that it did. Can that event be repeated and verified? No, but evolutionists believe it anyway — and pass it off as "science."

Dr. George Wald, a professor at Harvard University, in describing the "spontaneous" origin of life said that "time itself performs the miracles" (49). If the fortuitous commencement of life could occur (and there is absolutely no evidence that it did or can), such would have been a unique event.

The notion of "spontaneous generation," believed so vigorously by evolutionists, cannot be classified as "science." And since there were no "witnesses" to this alleged singular event, the idea is wholly void of any support.

"Spontaneous generation" is a philosophical "belief," not a scientific proposition.

The Checkered Past of Science

Any person who has a proper estimation of true science, cannot but be an admirer of those men and women who studied hard, who sacrificed selflessly, and who brought to us the numerous achievements in the domain of science by which we are so blessed today. But the historical reality is, along the way, that which has been called "science," has been littered with blunders of a colossal magnitude.

At various points in the past, superstition, sailing under the flag of science, taught: (1) the eternality of matter; (2) alchemy, the notion that common metals could be transformed into gold; (3) the spontaneous generation of life; (4) the recapitulation theory, i.e., the idea that during the nine-month gestation period the human embryo passes through the major stages of its evolutionary past; (5) the human body, with scores of so-called "vestigial" organs, is a museum of our evolutionary history; (7) the "steady state" theory, i.e., that matter is being continuously created; (8) the geocentric theory, the notion that the sun revolves around the earth; (9) the earth is flat; the contemporaries of Columbus believed he would sail off the edge of our planet; (10) the earth is supported by solid pillars; (11) the inheritance of "acquired" characteristics; (12) the preformation theory, the notion that in every woman's ova are complete human beings in miniature format; (13) departed wicked souls inhabit the interior of the earth; (14) the human brain is composed of "earth;" (15) astrology, the idea that the planets determine human destiny, etc., etc.

All these embarrassments, and others too numerous

to detail, should remind us that some, who have posed as "scientists," have been the most gullible, egotistical people on earth. To suggest that their pontifications must be taken with a grain of salt is to express it mildly. The most astounding thing of all, however, is the fact that the Holy Scriptures, though composed over a span of some sixteen centuries, never endorsed a single one of these baseless theories!

Conclusion

In view of these facts about how science works, its limitations, and its history, it ought to be very clear that not everything today that is called "science" actually is — in the legitimate sense of that term. We need not, therefore, be intimidated by the wild assertions that "science" disproves the existence of God, or "science" undermines faith. Science simply cannot deal with such matters, and we must not allow ourselves to be mesmerized by powerful sounding words, intimidating personalities, and the superficial pronouncements of the news media.

Questions

1. Give the best, one-word definition of "science" that you can.

2. Expand your definition slightly.

3. Name three categories sometimes assigned to "science."

4. Explain why the matter of "origins" does not come within the scope of "science."

5. Though it is commonly called the "theory of evolution," explain why the evolutionary concept actually does not meet

the standard of a credible theory.

6. List the stages in the "scientific method."

7. What are some of the limitations of science?

8. Discuss the statements of Louis More and J.W.N. Sullivan about the range of scientific inquiry. Did these respected scientists allow for "truth" beyond that which can be determined by the scientific method?

9. Can modern science determine whether or not Jesus Christ performed miracles? If not, explain why.

10. Discuss some of the historical "blunders" of the scientific community.

References

Bales, James D. (1976), *Evolution And The Scientific Method* (Searcy, AR: Bales).

Curtis, Helena (1975), *Biology* (New York: Worth Publishers).

Danson, R. (1971), *New Scientist*, Vol. 49.

Dawkins, Richard (1986), *The Blind Watchmaker* (New York: W.W. Norton & Co.).

Gould, Stephen J. (1999), *Time*, August 23.

Graham, E.G. (1965), *The Basic Dictionary of Science* (New York: The Macmillan Co).

More, Louis T. (1925), *The Dogma of Evolution* (Princeton: Princeton University).

Packard, Vance (1968), *The Sexual Wilderness* (New York: David McKay Co.).

Sullivan, J.W.N. (1940), *The Limitations of Science* (New York: Mentor).

Wald, George (1954), "The Origin of Life," *Scientific American*, Vol. 191, August.

CHAPTER 2

IS THE BIBLE SCIENTIFICALLY CREDIBLE?

There are various views that people entertain regarding the Bible. Some hold it to be strictly a human document — respectable with age, but certainly not an inspired revelation from God. They merely consider it as one of the great literary efforts of antiquity, much as the works of Plato or Shakespeare.

Others feel that the Scriptures have some sense of "divinity," but they do not believe that the Bible is entirely the Word of God. It may contain sacred truth, they allege, but it also has an admixture of purely human ideology. They would contend, therefore, that much of the Bible's history is flawed, and certainly it is "scientifically" antiquated. Neither of these views is consistent with the Bible's claim for itself. "All scripture is inspired of God . . ." (2 Tim. 3:16-17).

Many Bible students, including this writer, happily acknowledge that the Scriptures are verbally inspired — the infallible word of God. We are confident, as a result of careful and sustained study, that whenever the Bible touches upon a subject, it is accurate — if its language is truly understood. If God is the Author of nature, and if He is the Source of the Scriptures, the two will be in harmony, for He is not a deity of confusion (1 Cor. 14:33).

Our focus in this chapter, then, is this: Is the Bible accurate from a *scientific* standpoint?

The Bible: Not a Book of Science

It is frequently said that "the Bible is not a book of science." There is, of course, some truth in that. The Scriptures were not designed to set forth the law of gravity nor to explain that water is composed of two gases — oxygen and hydrogen. It is generally the case, though, when such a statement is made, that the author of it intends to convey the impression that the Bible is scientifically vulnerable; that it contains, in fact, outmoded "scientific" data. That simply is not the case.

While it technically is true that the Scriptures are not a textbook on science matters, when they *incidentally* touch on issues that relate to a scientific theme, we have every right to expect that the sacred documents will be without error. For example, it is also true that the Bible is "not a book of mathematics." It does not teach us how to add, subtract, or do fractions. Nevertheless, when it does discuss numbers, we expect it to be mathematically accurate. In Daniel's prophecy of the coming Messiah, he predicted that certain events would be fulfilled in "seventy" weeks; the sum was then segmented into sixty-two, seven, and one (Dan. 9:25-27). These figures add up to seventy. We do not expect a math "mistake" in such instances. We ought not, therefore, to be distracted by the meaningless quip: "The Bible is not a textbook on science."

The Bible's Scientific Precision

It is an amazing fact that though it was completed some twenty centuries ago, the biblical record is always consistent with the discoveries of science. This certainly cannot be said for any modern textbook dealing with scientific issues. Current science books will be obsolete within a very brief time.

When George Gamow published the 2nd edition of his book, *Biography of the Earth* in 1948, he had to write a special preface correcting errors in the first edition, because, as he noted, "many changes have taken place [during the past seven years] in our ideas concerning the origin of the planetary system." (He still had a galaxy of errors in that work.) Consider some of the following points:

(1) Many have argued (and some still do) that the universe is eternal; there never was a time when it did not exist. But Moses wrote: "In the beginning God created the heavens and the earth" (Gen. 1:1). But, as Dr. Robert Jastrow has pointed out: "Modern science denies an eternal existence to the Universe. . ." (15). This is one of the clear implications of the Second Law of Thermodynamics. Everything is "running down." It must have been, therefore, "wound up" at some point in the past.

(2) The book of Genesis states that Jehovah's creative activity concluded with the sixth day of the initial week (2:1-2). Accordingly, there is no creation of "matter" being effected today. This is perfectly consistent with the First Law of Thermodynamics, which asserts that according to present processes, matter is not being created now (which further suggests that it cannot *create itself*). It may be altered in form (e.g., from a solid to a gas), but it is neither being created nor destroyed.

Yet contrast these facts with the contention of Bertrand Russell — just forty-five years ago: "There is no reason why the world could not have come into being without a cause; nor, on the other hand, is there any reason why it should not have always existed" (7). These statements are absolutely absurd, and no self-respecting intellectual would echo them today. But the Bible is wonderfully current.

(3) Consider Paul's statement in his address to the philosophers of Athens. ". . . He [God] made of one every nation of men to dwell on all the face of the earth . . ." (Acts 17:26 ASV). The expression "of one" translates the Greek *ek henos*, literally "out of one male." The word "blood" (KJV) does not appear in the older Greek texts. And so, the inspired apostle affirmed that the entire human family was descended from one man, Adam.

This asserts the unity of humanity — contrary to ancient Greek ideology. The Athenians claimed to be an indigenous people — a special creation, and all others were considered barbarian (cf. Rom. 1:14).

This idea has its modern counterpart as well. Charles Darwin, the "father" of modern evolutionism, argued that the "Caucasian races" are superior, and from this concept Adolf Hitler developed his notion of the "master" race. As late as World War II, the U.S. Red Cross segregated blood (for transfusion purposes) according to race types. It is now scientifically known that there is a basic physical unity shared by all ethnic families of the earth.

Evolutionary anthropologist Dr. Ashley Montague has written that "all the ethnic groups of man must have originated from a single ancestral stock." He says "the more we study the different groups of man the more alike they turn out to be" (184). Again, the Bible proved true after all!

Alleged Inaccuracies

Unbelievers charge, however, that there are scientific blunders in the Scriptures — which ought not to be there if the narrative was given by God. Here are a few examples generally cited.

(1) In Genesis 1:6 Moses wrote: "And God said, Let there be a *firmament* in the midst of the waters . . ." (KJV). It is argued that this passage suggests there is a *firm* vault in the heavens that holds back the waters. There is a mistaken notion here alright, but it can be traced back to the Septuagint (Greek version of the Old Testament - from the 3rd century B.C.). Those translators were influenced by the ideas of their day in their rendition of the original term. However, the Hebrew word *raqiya* simply means an "expanse" (cf. NASB), and it does not imply a "solid" sky.

(2) We are told that the Bible contains references to the "unicorn," a mere mythical animal (cf. Num. 23:22 KJV). If the Scriptures are inspired, surely, it is charged, they would not embody such absurdities. Again, though, it is a matter of an inaccurate translation. It is now known that the Hebrew word *re'em,* in this context, refers to a species of extinct wild ox, and not to the legendary "unicorn."

(3) Some allege that the Scriptures contain a scientific blunder when they refer to the "four corners of the earth" (cf. Rev. 7:1). Supposedly, this is a mistake from

those days when unenlightened man believed the earth was flat. But the biblical phrase is simply a figurative expression for the *extremities* of the earth. Some time back the U.S. Marine Corps published a brochure affirming that this branch of the military has men "serving the flag at the four corners of the earth." Does anyone suggest that our government does not know the shape of the earth?

In addition we must mention that Isaiah spoke of God as sitting about the "circle of the earth" (40:22). Scholars have pointed out that the Hebrew word for "circle" (*chuwg*) "is compatible with the notion of the earth as a sphere" (Archer, 637). These examples could be multiplied several times over.

False Science Not in the Bible

Invariably, writings that are strictly "human" in composition reflect the "science" of their day. This is why, even today, science books have to be revised and rewritten every few years. It would be unthinkable to use a science text published just ten years ago. "Science" changes, and yesterday's science is frequently today's *superstition!*

It is an amazing thing that the Bible does not incorporate into its records the pseudo-science of the antique world. Surely this is evidence of its divine character. But consider the following — by way of contrast:

(1) Aristotle, the great Greek philosopher, said that the brain is a "compound of earth and water." He further taught that the human brain "is larger in men than in women." It isn't. He suggested that the "region of the

heart in man is hotter" than in animals (Chapter 7). The truth is, most birds and many mammals have warmer internal heat than humans.

(2) In the famous *Papyrus Ebers*, a medical text written in Egypt in the 16th century B.C., there is a prescription to prevent losing one's hair: "When it falls out, one remedy is to apply a mixture of six fats, namely those of the horse, hippopotamus, the crocodile, the cat, the snake, and the ibex. To strengthen it, anoint with the tooth of a donkey crushed in honey" (quoted by McMillen, 11).

Though Moses was raised in Egypt and was "instructed in all the wisdom of the Egyptians" (Acts 7:22), when he penned the Pentateuch (the first five books of the Bible), he incorporated no antique superstition into his narrative. In fact, that Old Testament narrative is astoundingly ahead of its time. The sanitation regulations, incorporated into certain portions of the Pentateuch (which presuppose the existence of "germs") cannot be explained except by the fact that God was behind the message.

Conclusion

When one argues that the Bible is scientifically flawed, or, in an attempt to compromise the integrity of scripture, flippantly quips: "Oh, the Bible is not a book of science," the Christian must rise to a defense of the flawless character of the sacred record.

Questions

1. Describe some of the views that people entertain concerning the nature of the Bible.

2. What claim does Scripture make for itself, in terms of its origin?

3. The statement is frequently made: "The Bible is not a book of science." What is right about that statement? What could be wrong about that statement?

4. If the Scriptures contain factual errors in matters of science, history, etc., can one have confidence in their *spiritual* instruction?

5. Cite some examples of how Genesis 1 is in harmony with scientific law.

6. What is the significance of Paul's affirmation regarding the unity of the human family (Acts 17:26)?

7. Is the Old Testament accurate when it mentions the "unicorn" (KJV)? Where does the problem lie?

8. Did biblical writers endorse the notion of a "flat" earth? Explain.

9. How are the writings of Moses different from those produced in Egypt during the time he was growing up?

References

Archer, Gleason (1963), "Isaiah," *The Wycliffe Bible Commentary*, Charles Pfeiffer & Everett Harrison, Eds. (London: Oliphants).

Aristotle (1943 ed.), "Parts of Animals," *On Man And The Universe* (Roslyn, NY: Walter J. Black, Inc.).

Gamow, George (1948), *Biography of the Earth* (New York: Mentor).

Jastrow, Robert (1980), *Until The Sun Dies* (New York: Warner).

McMillen, S.I. (1963), *None Of These Diseases* (Westwood, NJ: Fleming H. Revell Co.).

Montague, Ashley (1960), *Human Heredity* (New York: Mentor Books).

Russell, Bertrand (1957), *Why I Am Not A Christian and Other Essays* (New York: Simon & Schuster).

CHAPTER 3

THE BIBLE AND ASTRONOMY

"And God said, Let there be lights in the expanse of heaven to divide the day from the night; and let them be for signs, and for seasons, and for days and years: and let them be for lights in the expanse of heaven to give light upon the earth: and it was so. And God made the two great lights: the greater light to rule the day, and the lesser light to rule the night: he made the stars also" (Genesis 1:14-16).

The word "astronomy" derives from two roots — *astron,* "star" and *nomos,* "law." The word suggests an arrangement or distribution of the stars. This, in itself, implies a law-giver or an arranger. The Greeks called the universe *cosmos* (not *chaos*), suggesting order. The Bible itself speaks of the "ordinances" of the heavens (Jer. 31:35). It is a fundamental principle of logic that where there is law, there must be a law-giver. The U.S. Constitution did not compose itself! The law-giver, the orderer of the universe, is its Creator, God.

More formally stated, astronomy is the science of the study of the stars, planets, etc., together with their movements and relations to one another. Originally, this "science" was steeped in superstition (astrology); it is only in relatively recent times that it has gained scientific respectability. And even now, it is woefully afflicted with evolutionary baggage.

The Origin of Heavenly Luminaries

Basically, there are two views of the origin of the universe. It occurred either *naturally*, or its commencement was *supernatural*. The question is: To which concept does the evidence point?

The common view today is that the universe resulted from the "Big Bang." It is suggested that all the matter then in existence (which supposedly dates to some 20 billion years ago) "was compressed into an infinitely dense and hot mass" (called a "cosmic egg") that finally exploded (about 10 billion years ago), thus producing the ordered systems of the universe (Jastrow, 2-3). According to an article in *National Geographic*, the "egg" was "many billions of times smaller than a single proton" (705). Where this "egg" came from, no one seems to know. Certainly no "cosmic chicken" has yet been located! There are, however, many problems with the Big Bang theory. Consider just two of them.

(1) As noted already, the Greeks called the universe the *cosmos*, meaning "order," because it is so precisely mechanistic — like a brilliantly designed, well-regulated machine. No mere "explosion" could have occasioned this machine. A blowup in a printing factory does not produce an encyclopedia. A stack of lumber and dynamite cannot construct a house. But ". . . every house is built by someone; but the builder of all things is God" (Heb. 3:4 NASB). Intelligence can fashion a habitable dwelling; mere force cannot. And so, "accident" is not an adequate explanation for an ordered system. Henri Poincare (1854-1912), considered to be one of the greatest mathematicians and original thinkers of his day,

declared: "The world is divine because it is a harmony" (Young, 135).

(2) An explosion propels objects radially — in all directions. If one lights a firecracker on the driveway, following the denotation, the distribution of the paper fragments will give a clear idea of the effects of a "bang" — and there will be no discernible order. The planets of our solar system are characterized by spinning and curving motions (e.g., in orbits), with lovely balance. This marvelous arrangement argues for design, not randomness.

For further study, see the feature article, "The Big Bang" (December, 1999) on our web site - http://www.christiancourier.com.

Astronomy and Design

As suggested above, a study of the heavenly luminaries reveals that the universe was "put together" in a well-orchestrated way. A recognition of this "harmony" is the foundation of scientific investigation. Let us illustrate this point.

David, the great psalmist, a thousand years before the birth of Christ, declared: "The heavens declare the glory of God and the firmament [expanse NASB] showeth his handiwork" (Psa. 19:1) The starry hosts of the heavens testify concerning God in two ways. The vastness of the expanse is a commentary on his *power*. The organization is testimony to his *intelligence*. Let us briefly think about these two matters.

First, the number of heavenly bodies within the universe is beyond our ability to comprehend. Primitive astronomers tried to number the stars. In 150 B.C., Hipparchus estimated there were less than 3,000 stars. Three centuries later, Ptolemy suggested a slightly larger figure. One of the latest estimates today is that there could be as many as 100 septillion stars in space (that's a one followed by twenty-six zeros). And Albert Einstein suggested that the totality of space could be as much as 100,000 times greater than *known* space (Boyd, 289). All the while, though, the Scriptures had taught that the stars are numberless (Gen. 13:16; Jer. 33:22). And God knows them all by name (Psa. 147:4). What power has the Maker of this universe!

Second, David described the starry hosts as Jehovah's "handiwork," indeed, the exquisite work of his "fingers" (Psa. 8:3). Job exclaimed that the heavens were "garnished" by the Creator (Job 26:13). The original term is a feminine form suggesting "fairness, beauty, brilliancy." A New Testament writer says the "worlds" were "framed" by the word of God (Heb. 11:3). Reflect upon some of the design features of the Lord's universe.

(1) Our earth is the third planet from the sun (93 million miles away). It is spinning on its axis at the rate of 1,000 miles per hour (at the equator). Too, the earth is moving in an elliptical orbit around the sun at an average speed of 66,600 m.p.h. It travels 595 million miles in its yearly route around the "track." Here is a good question: What started this movement? There is no *natural* explanation. Sir Isaac Newton's First Law of Motion asserts that a stationary object will remain so until force is exerted upon it from some other source. This fact has forced many philosophers and logicians to postulate a

"Prime Mover." The Bible calls Him "God."

(2) The earth is delicately balanced in its orbit. As the earth moves around the sun, centrifugal force pushes it outward (much like a weight attached to a string and whirled above your head). At the same time, the force of gravity pulls it toward the sun. It has been estimated that it would take a steel cable at least 8,000 miles in diameter (comparable to that of our earth) to equal the strength of the force which ties this planet to the sun (Stoner, 55). Gravity! What a mysterious force. We constantly see its effect, but still do not understand it. We can explain the principle of its universal force, but we really do not even know what it is.

> The very law which molds a tear,
>   And bids it trickle from its source,
> That law preserves the earth a sphere,
>   And guides the planets in their course.
> *Samuel Rogers*

The amazing balance between these forces of nature can be explained reasonably only in the light of intelligent design.

(2) Some scientists refer to the "mathematical orthodoxy" of the universe. In his book, *The Universe and Dr. Einstein*, Lincoln Barnett talks about the "functional harmony" of the universe (22). Think about this. As the earth travels in its orbit around the sun, it must make minute adjustments to conform to its elliptical "track." Our planet digresses from a straight line one-ninth of an inch every eighteen miles. If the modification was only a

tenth of an inch, our globe would gradually move toward outer space and eventually become a frozen ball. If the adjustment was as much as one-eighth of an inch, we would be pulled toward the sun and finally incinerated. The balance is just right.

If not for the mathematical precision of the universe, how could astronomers predict eclipses? How could space scientists target satellites with such pinpoint accuracy? Consider this interesting bit of history. Prior to the year 1846, the planet Neptune was unknown to earth's astronomers. It is too far away (2,800 million miles) to be seen with the naked eye. In the early 1800's, two scientists, John Adams in Great Britain, and Jean Leverrier in France, working independently, had noticed strange behavior in the orbital movements of the planet Uranus. They surmised that perhaps the gravitational pull of some unknown planet was affecting Uranus. Working strictly "on paper" with mathematical calculations, each man — unaware of the other's labor — predicted where the invisible planet ought to be. In 1846, Johann Galle of the Berlin Observatory made a search for the hidden body. He discovered it less than one degree from the predicted location. What eloquent testimony to the "mathematical orthodoxy" of the universe. Who was the great Mathematician who put it all together?

One unbelieving scientist, Dr. Edward Friedkin, a physicist, has confessed: "It's hard for me to believe that everything out there is just an accident . . . it seems likely to me that this particular universe we have is a consequence of something which I would call intelligent" (Wright, 69).

The Purpose of Heavenly Luminaries

Why did God create the sun, the moon, and the stars? Most of them are far beyond man's ability to visit, even if a human could survive there. If one wanted to draw a map of our universe, with a scale of 1 inch = 93 million miles (the distance from earth to the sun), his paper would have to be four miles long to include our next nearest star. The map would need to be 25,000 miles long just to reach to the center of the Milky Way galaxy!

Moses described the purpose of the planets and stars in Genesis 1. They were designed to "divide the day from the night," to be for "signs, and for seasons, and for days and years," and to serve in the expanse to "give light upon the earth" (1:14-15).

The sun provides light (and heat) upon the earth for the day time. It is called the "greater" light (compared to the moon); it is significant that the inspired writer did not say, the "greatest" light (as the sun would have appeared to the ordinary observer fifteen centuries before Christ), for there are many stars larger than the sun.

The rotation of our earth upon its axis, in relation to the sun, produces the day-night sequence. The revolution of the earth in its orbit around the sun, each 365 days, measures the year. The inclination of the earth on its axis, relative to the sun, provides our seasons, which facilitate the growing of crops.

For many centuries the stars have served as material "signs," i.e., navigational devices for the mariner. On their dangerous voyage to Rome, Luke notes that the inmates of the ship were unable to see either sun or stars for many days, hence, knew not where they were (Acts 27:20). Moreover, the constellations Pleides and Orion (Job 38:31) make their appearances in the spring and fall respectively, thus heralding the coming of these seasons.

Further, the Lord has made use of celestial bodies as "signs" for the teaching of *spiritual* lessons. When Joseph dreamed of the sun, moon, and stars bowing down to him (Gen. 37), it was a prophetic symbol of his future glory. Balaam's prophecy of a "star" to come out of Jacob (Num. 24:17), is most likely a preview of the coming of Christ, who refers to himself as "the bright and morning star" (Rev. 22:16). Perhaps it is significant that the wise men from the east, who followed the star to Bethlehem, may have been from the same region where Balaam himself had lived.

When the Israelites went to battle against a coalition of pagan tribes, God caused the sun to stop in the middle of the sky, where it hastened not to go down for about a whole day (cf. Josh. 10:13 NASB). Though skeptics dismiss this account as purely mythical, and liberals attempt to find naturalistic explanations, the conservative scholar accepts the event as a miracle, possibly a localized refraction of light (Davis/Whitcomb, 69), as an evidence of God's presence with his people. Certainly that day was unique in the annals of earth history (cf. Josh. 10:14).

God employed some sort of heavenly light ("star" — a generic term) to guide the wise men to the place where the infant Christ lay (Mt. 2:2, 9). This phenomenon cannot be explained save by a miracle.

Conclusion

The sun, moon, and stars are magnificent evidences of the Creator's genius and power. They are both aesthetic and functional. Dr. Arthur Harding, Professor of Mathematics and Astronomy at the University of Arkansas, wrote:

> As we look at the machines in some of our factories we sometimes wonder at what the mind of man has created, overlooking the fact that we are living on a little world that is a part of a gigantic machine which is operating silently and everlastingly in the sky . . . . Surely here is a gigantic machine which makes us stand in awe and wonder at the power of the creator who could design such a machine and put it into operation (67).

Unfortunately, over the centuries, some have given the heavenly bodies undue prominence. It is an interesting fact that whereas the ancient heathen gave much attention to the sun, moon, and stars — even worshipping them — the Hebrews were not preoccupied with such matters, doubtless due to prohibition against star worship, etc. (cf. Dt. 4:19; 17:2-5; Isa. 47:13; Jer. 44:19).

Modern devotees of astrology (who allege that the sky's luminaries have control over the destinies of men) are equally pagan.

Truly, the heavens do declare the glory of God (Psa. 19:1ff).

Questions

1. Define the term "astronomy." What does the etymology of the word imply?

2. Cite two logical flaws in the "Big Bang" idea.

3. What two elements of God's nature are illustrated by the starry hosts of the heavens?

4. What was Newton's First Law of Motion?

5. What are the two forces that stabilize the earth in its relationship to the sun?

6. Illustrate "mathematical orthodoxy" in the universe.

7. List some of the "purposes" of the heavenly luminaries.

8. Discuss the implications of Prof. Harding's statement that the universe is a "gigantic machine."

9. What is the difference between "astronomy" and "astrology"?

10. What is God's view of the practice of astrology?

References

Barnett, Lincoln (1957), *The Universe and Dr. Einstein* (New York: Mentor Books).

Boyd, Robert (1983), *World's Bible Handbook* (Iowa Falls: World).

Davis, John & Whitcomb, John (1970), *A History of Israel* (Grand Rapids: Baker Book House).

Harding, Arthur (1940), *Astronomy: The Splendor of the Heavens Brought Down to Earth* (New York: Garden City Publishing Co.).

Jackson, Wayne (1999), *The Big Bang* (December), www.christiancourier.com

Jastrow, Robert (1977), *Until The Sun Dies* (New York: Warner).

National Geographic, June, 1983.

Stoner, Peter (1963), *Science Speaks* (Chicago: Moody Press).

Wright, Robert (1988), *Three Scientists and Their Gods* (New York: Harper & Row).

Young, Louise B., Ed. (1971), *Exploring the Universe* (New York: Oxford University Press).

CHAPTER 4

THE BIBLE AND OCEANOGRAPHY

"And God said, Let the waters under the heavens be gathered together unto one place, and let the dry land appear: and it was so. And God called the dry land Earth; and the gathering together of the waters called he Seas: and God saw that it was good" (Gen. 1:9-10).

Another biblical writer, centuries before Christ, spoke of the wonders of earth's vast sea. "Those who go down to the sea in ships, Who do business on great waters; They have seen the works of the Lord, And His wonders in the deep" (Psa. 107:23-24 NASB). Wonders indeed.

Water, Water, Everywhere

Before we discuss the seas, it is not out of place that we say just a word about water itself. It was a part of earth's environment on the first day of the creation week.

". . . . [T]he Spirit of God moved upon the face of the waters" (Gen. 1:2).

Water is so important that life could not exist without it. Actually, water is a combination of two gases. When two atoms of hydrogen unite with one atom of oxygen, water is formed. (Incidentally, atoms are incredibly small. If one could enlarge an atom to the size of a pin-head, the atoms in one grain of sand would make a cube 1 mile x 1 mile x 1 mile.) The chemical mixture has to be just right for water to exist. Water can exist in three forms — liquid, solid (ice), and gas (steam). No other substance appears in these three forms within earth's normal range of temperature.

The properties of water are such that it graciously accommodates the world of living creatures. It has the powerful ability to dissolve almost any substance. For instance, water dissolves nutrients in the soil and transports them to plants. This precious liquid dissolves the food that we eat, and carries it to the cells throughout the body. In fact, the human body is about 65% water. We need more than two quarts of water each day (in some form or another) to assist our body with its various functions.

Water also possesses what is known as the capillarity feature. This is its ability to climb up a surface against the pull of gravity. One can put a piece of absorbent string in a pan of water and drape it over the edge. The water will climb the string and drip from the tip at the opposite end. This phenomenon helps water circulate through the soil and up the roots of plants. What an amazing gift God has provided in water!

Earth's Seas

In relatively recent times, the science of oceanography has thrown a floodlight on the amazing nature of our planet's seas. Further, there is astounding agreement between the ancient biblical text and the modern science of oceanography.

Oceanography is the study of the history, geography, motions, and chemical composition of that large body of water that bathes a considerable portion of the earth's surface.

Design in the Deep

On the second day of the creation week, God compartmentalized the waters of the earth. Some were housed in the atmosphere, above the expanse. This blanket of vapor enclosed the earth and almost certainly was the phenomenon that produced a pre-Flood greenhouse-like effect. There is ample evidence that once there was a universally mild climate upon the earth.

Other waters were stored on the surface of the globe — and even beneath the surface (Gen. 1:6-7). Subsequently, Jehovah gathered the waters on earth's surface under the heavens into "one place," and yet He called them "Seas" (Gen. 1:9-10). Two things are important here.

First, science recognizes that "ocean" designates "the great body of salt water covering over 70% of the earth," and that there are "five divisions" which are recognized by the placements of certain land masses (Graham, 289). The Genesis record accurately depicts the current arrangement of land and water, though we must acknowledge that the distribution was obviously somewhat different in the pre-Flood world (cf. Peter's reference to "the world that then was," 2 Pet. 3:6).

Second, with Moses' limited range of activity, he could hardly have known, on his own, of the planet's various "Seas." This evidences the revelatory nature of his record.

But let us take brief note of some of the evidences of design in our globe's great bodies of water — those things which make them "good."

(1) As indicated above, slightly more than 70% of the planet's surface is covered by water. Surely if man had designed his environment, the land-water ratio would have been very different. But the respective proportions are very significant. The oceans' waters are the primary source of the life-giving rains that water the globe. Based upon certain mathematical calculations, it is suggested that if the global ocean was half its present capacity, the earth would receive only a fourth of its current average rainfall, and the planet would virtually be a desert. On the other hand, if the ocean covered a half more of the present land mass, than it now does, the annual rainfall would be four times its current capacity, and the globe would be a massive swamp. There is a "just right" balance.

(2) Every school child knows that ocean water is salty. Every gallon of seawater contains about a quarter of a pound of salt. It has been estimated that if all the ocean's salt were extracted and spread over the surface of the earth, it would cover the surface of our planet with a layer some 400 feet thick.

This saltiness of the ocean appears to reflect design on the part of the Creator. In his fascinating book, *The*

Universe: Plan Or Accident?, Dr. Robert E.D. Clark notes that water vapor *alone* does not readily lend itself to the production of clouds. "Nuclei," he says, "must be provided on which the water can condense." The huge quantities of salt in the seas, together with wind and water action, create the conditions whereby the formation of rain is generally made available over the surface of the earth (75-76).

Rains produce lakes and rivers which pour water back into the sea. "It has been calculated that if no water were returned to the ocean by precipitation or by rivers from the land, the whole ocean would be dried up in from three thousand to four thousand years" (Price, 354). This system, involving *evaporation* (an amazing process since water weighs 800 times more than air), *transportation* across the land, and *condensation* (approximately 16 million tons per second world wide) is called the hydrologic cycle. It actually was not generally understood until the 16th and 17th centuries A.D. (Morton, 49). Yet, note Solomon's reference to the concept almost a thousand years before the birth of Jesus (cf. Eccl. 1:7). Further, Amos stated that God "calls for the waters of the sea, and pours them out upon the face of the earth" (5:8c).

(3) Since there is so much water upon the earth, it is amazing that our globe is not "baptized" in the delightful liquid. The fact is, if all of the planet's features were smoothed out, water would cover the entire earth to a depth of some two miles. But this is not the case, of course, because God has laid up "the deep in storehouses" (Psa. 33:7; cf. "channels of the deep," 2 Sam. 22:16). There is far greater depth to the ocean than there is

height to the land. If earth's highest mountain (Everest) were placed in the lowest known depression of the ocean (called Challenger Deep), the water would stand a mile above Everest's peak!

Dr. A. Cressy Morrison, who was a fellow of the American Museum of Natural History, and a life member of the Royal Institution of Great Britain, and who accepted many of the tenets of Darwinism, called earth's ocean "the great balance wheel" upon which the life of the planet is dependent (23).

Twelve Treasures of the Sea

After Jehovah had made the seas, Moses notes that he assessed his work as "good" (Gen. 1:10). The adjective in the Hebrew text has a variety of meanings; among these, it can denote that which is "pleasant" or "beautiful," or that which produces "well-being." Certainly the seas evince both beauty and value. Let us reflect upon some of the treasures of the sea.

(1) Some 13% of our salt needs are supplied by the seas. Humans need salt to survive; this chemical compound makes up about 0.9% of our blood and cells.

(2) The sea provides numerous minerals. A cubic mile of sea water has about 4 million tons of magnesium, and most of our magnesium derives from the sea. This lightest of all metals is used in the human body to activate enzymes, and is employed by scientists in the manufacture of many of the items we use every day e.g., airplanes, electronic equipment, etc. Moreover, it is estimated that each cubic mile of the ocean's water contains

about $90 million worth of gold.

(3) The oceans are like giant highways that accommodate worldwide travel and commerce. Even ancient Tyre, with her fleets, was said to be the "merchant of the people unto many islands" (Ezek. 27:3).

(4) The world's great seas provide millions of dollars worth of food to feed earth's rapidly growing population.

(5) The ocean yields its moisture for rains to facilitate the growing of crops upon the bosom of mother earth.

(6) Oil, gas, and sulfur are pumped in swelling torrents from the sea floor.

(7) There are vast deposits of iron, copper, cobalt, and nickel at the bottom of the sea. These doubtless will be mined increasingly in the future.

(8) Because water has a high specific heat capacity, the vast expanses of the seas work effectively to create more equitable temperatures on the earth, than would be the case otherwise if earth's land mass was greater.

(9) The tremendous currents (e.g., the Gulf Stream - a thousand times wider than the size of the Mississippi river at its mouth) produce many valuable benefits, such as moderating climate, facilitating shipping, and enhancing the fishing industry.

(10) It is estimated that 90% of the oxygen we breathe comes from one-celled plants and seaweed in the ocean.

(11) With all of the chemicals and minerals that are annually washed into the seas, it is surprising that the waters are not highly contaminated. But, as Dr. Alan

Hayward, one of Great Britain's scientists, has observed, there "appear to be a number of automatic control systems" (somewhat analogous to a thermostat) that keep the chemical composition of the ocean stabilized (67).

(12) Every day, twice a day (approximately every twelve hours and twenty-six minutes), the ocean's tides (produced by the moon's attraction) become high and low. These tides are of enormous benefit in sweeping our harbors and bays, which, in connection with large cities, would otherwise quickly become health hazards. Tides also assist in keeping channels clear for navigation.

Scientific Foreknowledge and the Seas

Dr. Henry Morris once wrote: "One of the most arresting evidences of the inspiration of the Bible is the great number of scientific truths that have lain hidden within its pages for thirty centuries or more, only to be discovered by man's enterprise within the last few centuries or even years" (5). Since a number of these are related to the sea, we will consider a few of them.

(1) Ancient biblical writers often used expressions relative to the topography of the sea floor that they could not have known by natural investigation in those days before the scientific study of the ocean floor. Several Bible passages refer to the "deep places" (Psa. 135:6), or the "channels of the deep" (2 Sam. 22:16; cf. Psa. 18:15-16), and also to the "mountains" underneath the sea (Jon. 2:5-6). Several modern encyclopedias now have maps of suboceanic mountain ranges. There is a massive range off the eastern coast of the United States.

A.E. Parr, who served as the director of the American Museum of Natural History, wrote: "Before the invention of echo-sounding equipment it was generally thought that the bottom of the oceans would present the appearance of plains, plateaus and gently rolling terrain. Now we know that it also has valleys and mountain ranges, and even canyons, to equal all the forms we find on land" (580). Incredibly, even at this point, we know more about the surface of the moon than we do the bottom of the ocean.

(2) When the Lord wanted to show a rather critical Job how very little the patriarch actually knew about earth's environment, he asked: "Have you entered into the springs of the deep?" (Job 38:16). The earliest reference to such submarine springs dates to the time of Strabo (63 B.C. - 21 A.D.). It is now known that fresh water springs are found in a number of regions of the ocean. For example, there are several sources in the Atlantic — from New England to Georgia (Morton, 115).

(3) A thousand years before Christ's birth, David, in a psalm extolling the glory of God as reflected in the creation, referred to that which "passes through the paths of the sea" (Psa. 8:8). Matthew Fontaine Maury (1806-73) is generally credited with being the first to chart the sea's "paths." An inscription on the Maury monument characterizes this scientist as "the pathfinder of the seas." He sought to find that to which Israel's shepherd king alluded almost two millennia earlier. How could David have known about the "paths of the sea"? Incredible!

The Ocean and Evolution

One of the strong arguments against the theory of evolution is this: There simply has not been enough time for the protracted process of amoeba-to-man to have occurred. Even the followers of Darwin concede: No time — no evolution! Time is the "hero of the plot."

It is estimated that more than 2 billion tons of sediment are dumped from rivers into the oceans each year. Add other factors to this (e.g., the flow of ground water, shoreline erosion, etc.), and it is projected that all of earth's continents would completely erode away in some 14 million years (Nevins, i-iv). An evolutionary source expresses bafflement regarding this: "Why, in the course of millennia, is there so astonishingly little sediment on the ocean floor?" (Platt, 125). The answer? Because the time postulated by evolutionary chronology is simply not there! (see our book, *Creation, Evolution, and the Age of the Earth*).

Conclusion

A consideration of the Bible, in light of the growing science of oceanography, leaves the Scriptures perfectly respectable! Moreover, the blessings and wonders of the sea are a vivid commentary on the love and benevolence of the Creator for His creatures upon this planet.

Questions

1. Name two properties of water that illustrate its value in the accommodation of life on earth.

2. What is the land-to-water ratio of this planet?

3. Why is a proper water-land balance important for earth?

4. What is significant about the fact that Moses, in Genesis 1, mentions "seas" (plural), and yet says the waters were gathered together in "one place"?

5. What is the value of salt in producing rain?

6. Describe the movements of the "hydrologic" cycle. Site a biblical passage that alludes to this process.

7. Since earth's water surface is more than twice that of the land, how is it that the land is not swamped with water?

8. Discuss the meaning of the term "good" in Genesis 1:10.

9. List some of the "treasures" of the seas.

10. Cite some examples of biblical information — related to the seas — that are far in advance of modern scientific discovery.

References

Parr, A.E. (1961), "Deep-Sea Life," *Encyclopedia Americana* (New York: Americana Corp.), Vol. 8.

Graham, E.C. (1965), *The Basic Dictionary of Science* (New York: The Macmillan Co.).

Hayward, Alan (1978), *God Is - A scientist shows why it is reasonable to believe in God* (Nashville: Thomas Nelson).

Morris, Henry M. (1968), *The Bible and Modern Science* (Chicago: Moody Press).

Morrison, A. Cressy (1944), *Man Does Not Stand Alone* (Westwood, NJ: Fleming H. Revell).

Morton, Jean Sloat (1978), *Science in the Bible* (Chicago: Moody).

Nevins, Stuart (1973), "Evolution: The Ocean Says No!," *ICR Impact Series,* October, No. 8.

Platt, Rutherford (1969), "Unearthly World at the Bottom of the Sea," *Our Amazing World of Nature* (Pleasantville, NY: Reader's Digest Association).

Price, George M. (n.d.), *A Textbook of General Science* (Mountain View, CA: Pacific Press).

CHAPTER 5

THE BIBLE AND GEOLOGY

Some theories are born, and they die fairly soon; scientific investigation kills them. It doesn't take long to reject the notion that a horse hair can turn into a worm when soaked in water. But other baseless views are more difficult to eradicate. Hypotheses concerning the formation of distant galaxies, or the precise composition of the earth's interior, linger on and on, simply because they cannot be subjected to the kind of scientific scrutiny that quickly discredits error. Such is largely the case with reference to the "science" of geology. This field of study deals with the distant past, fogged in obscurity, and it is saturated with reckless speculation.

Geology involves a study of the history of the earth, its composition, the forces that have worked upon it, and the remains of ancient plants and animals. It was a fledgling discipline until the advent of Darwinism; it then came into its own — as an alleged "biography of the earth," to borrow the title of George Gamow's book. Now, many claim that geology provides the "proof positive" that organic evolution has occurred. Others (even some evolutionists), are more reserved.

Earth's History: Two Views

There are two fundamental views of earth history. One is called *Uniformitarianism,* the other is designated as *Catastrophism*. The former is the evolutionary concept; the latter represents the biblical viewpoint. Let us consider these two ideologies briefly.

"Uniformitarianism" is the notion that the earth's features, as currently observed, are the result of *gradual* changes, over a very long period of time (supposedly, several billion years). Thus, the slow processes we see occurring now are a commentary on the forces of nature in the past. The favorite phrase in the evolutionary vocabulary is: *"The present is a key to the past."*

[Note: It is here that we meet with a major contradiction in the evolutionary scheme of things. In advocating his *geology,* the Darwinist claims that the operations of the earth have always been *uniform*. But in arguing his *biology* (attempting an explanation for the "spontaneous" origin of life), he alleges that earth's conditions were *different* in the past! (see Simpson, *et al.,* 1957, 263, 741).]

An alternate concept for explaining the earth's features is called "Catastrophism." This is the idea that the planet's surface has been subject to violent changes in the past — and on a worldwide scale. From the biblical vantage point, the most significant of these would be the global Flood of Noah's day.

The key question, then, is this: Which of these ideas best conforms with the actual *facts* of geology? That is the thrust of this study.

The Geologic Column

Before we begin our discussion of the facts revealed in the geologic strata, we must say a brief word about the so-called "geologic column" that appears in many geology and biology textbooks. It purports to show, in chart form, about twelve different geologic "ages," representing various life forms, as observed in the fossil record, beginning with the simple and moving toward the complex. What most people do not realize is this:

(1) That "column" exists nowhere on earth except on the paper of those books.

(2) It is a contrived construction based upon the presumption that evolution has occurred. Suppose we have several dominos scattered on a table. These will represent different strata (layers) of the earth with their respective fossils. How shall we organize these? If we assume that evolution has occurred — from the simple to the complex — we will stack the dominos accordingly, make a chart of them and publish it in a textbook! We need not be bothered by the fact that in the *real* fossil record, these layers are often all mixed up. The theory must take precedence over the facts!

(3) The "geologic timetable," as the column is sometimes called, is contradicted by numerous facts in the actual strata of the earth. For example, if all of the theoretical geologic records of earth's living creatures, that supposedly evolved over a span 2 of billion years, were stacked on top of one another (as in our domino illustration), the depth would be about 130 miles. Compare that with the fact that the earth's crust is only twenty-five to thirty miles deep!

We have thoroughly addressed this matter in our book, *The Mythology of Modern Geology.*

The Explosion of Life

One of the most amazing features of the geologic record is the fact that life forms virtually explode into existence. Dr. George Simpson of Harvard acknowledged that a great variety of organisms "are suddenly present" in the lower region of the geologic index (called the Cambrian Period). (This "index" is that artificially-arranged fossil column, referred to above.) Simpson calls this a "major mystery of the history of life" (1949, 18).

The truth is, every major invertebrate animal group has been found at the so-called Cambrian level — with no observable ancestors. But why is this such a mystery? Because if the theory of evolution were true, one would expect to see the different life forms sporadically and gradually appearing — with proliferation following. But that is not what the evidence reveals.

On the other hand, this circumstance is exactly what one would expect to discover as a consequence of the great Flood of Noah's time. The sedimentary (water-laid) strata that are the deepest would contain a vast number of simpler organisms — those that, due to lack of mobility and greater density (e.g., shelled creatures), would be buried more quickly in the upheaval of the Deluge.

The facts fit the biblical record much better.

The Complexity of Life Forms

Another aspect of geologic history, which even the evolutionists describe as "puzzling" (Kay/Colbert, 102), is the amazing complexity of the fossils in the Cambrian period. Consider, for instance, the little creature known as the "trilobite." It had eyes so complex that the math, explaining how the lens functioned, was not worked out until the last century! The trilobite is now extinct.

Incidentally, the issue for evolution is not exclusively, "how did all these creatures arrive?" — but, *where did they go?*

If evolution were the great fact of history, one should find fossilized organisms in various stages of development — from the incomplete to the complete — with the gaps filled in. But that is not the case; every organ and structure is complete. Not a single fossil has been discovered with half-formed features.

The Missing Links

We've all heard about "the missing link." That expression is a misrepresentation. It is not that there is a missing "link," it is a matter of missing "links" — *all of them* — between the major groups of earth's animals. This is true concerning creatures living upon the earth today, and it is equally true regarding those specimens buried in the fossil record. There are no provable "transitions." Evolutionary "geology" is "gap-ology."

The Genesis account affirms that the basic forms of biological life were created "after their kind" (Gen. 1:11ff). This statement is strictly at variance with the idea that all living creatures have descended, through natural processes, from a solitary, beginning life source — that fortuitously sprang into existence.

If the story of evolution were true, there should be,

in the earth's strata, a finely-graduated chain of evidence, with thousands of intermediate links between the major kinds of creatures. But the links are absent — because they never existed! In the various museums of the world, millions of fossil samples are on display, representing some 250,000 different species. And yet, the evolutionary "chain" still has the coveted "links" missing.

Charles Darwin was aware of this problem and confessed that this is "the most serious objection which can be urged against the theory" (313).

George Simpson of Harvard, affectionately dubbed "Mr. Evolution" by his admirers, conceded that there is a "regular absence of transitional forms" in the fossil record, and that such is a "universal phenomenon" — among both plants and animals (1944, 107).

Stephen Gould of Harvard, a leading defender of evolution today, says there is "precious little in the way of intermediate forms," and the "transitions between major groups are characteristically abrupt" (24). *But this is exactly what one would expect to find if the Genesis account is true!*

Perhaps this is why Mark Ridley, a professor of zoology at Oxford University, says that "no real evolutionist . . . uses the fossil record as evidence in favor of the theory of evolution as opposed to special creation" (830).

Demise of the Species

According to the theory of evolution, nature is endowed with marvelous and mysterious mechanisms for the creation and proliferation of living organisms. Supposedly, then, over the past 2 to 3 billion years, life forms have been exploding on the panoramic scene of history. If that view is true, one would expect a sparseness of fossils, the further back he proceeds in the fossil "biography." But this is not what the evidence reveals. It is believed that 98% of all creatures that have existed upon the earth now are extinct (Howard/Rifkin, 21). This doesn't fit with the story of evolution.

A Record of Degeneration

The evolutionary concept argues that by means of natural selection (the struggle in nature), animals that are more "fit" survive (Darwin's "survival of the fittest"), and the weak are eliminated. Ideally, then, species become hardier across the millennia. That, however, is hardly what the geologic evidence indicates.

Prior to the Flood the patriarchs lived many times longer than we now do (cf. Gen. 5:5, 27). By the time of Abraham, 175 was an "old age" (Gen. 25:7-8). Clay tablets from ancient Sumer (now southern Iraq) tell of kings who reigned fabulously long periods of time. While these texts contain obvious exaggerations, archaeologists contend "they may well be a legendary account of the fact revealed in the Bible that people did live to greater ages in early times" (Free/Vos, 38).

The same pattern of degeneration may be observed in the fossil history. "The fossils, regarded as a whole, invariably supply us with types larger of their kind and better developed in every way than their nearest modern representatives, whether of plants or animals" (Price,

206). Sir William Dawson said that *"degeneracy is the rule* rather than the exception" (quoted by Price, 211; org. emp). This circumstance is not even disputed. Some ancient locusts had a wingspan of over seven inches. Dragon flies had bodies a foot long. There were some frogs in the ancient world close to ten feet in length. The biblical record also hints of this degeneracy. The accelerating effect of sin has wrought a terrible price upon the earth and its inhabitants (see Rom. 5:12; 8:20ff).

Catastrophism and the Fossil Graveyards

It has been estimated that some 70% of the earth's strata are sedimentary (water-laid). This explains, in large part, why so many fossils have been preserved in the recesses of our planet. When a plant or animal dies, usually it is eaten by some other creature, or else it decays. "Only those [plants or animals] buried quickly and protected from decay can become fossils" (Welles, 364). Here is where the Genesis narrative and the evolution theory again come into serious conflict. As we noted earlier, Darwin's doctrine is based upon the doctrine of *Uniformitarianism,* that is, the *slow* processes now at work, according to evolutionary geologists, can "account for all the geologic features of the Globe" (Dunbar, 18).

But the truth is, the "biography of the earth" does not suggest that the fossils were laid down ever so slowly over vast periods of time. There are fossil graveyards in many areas of the world which contain the preserved remains of all sorts of creatures, wildly thrown together in massive burial sites, and quite obviously interred very quickly. Moreover, they are grossly distorted, suggesting that they died rather violently. In his book, *The Fundamentals of Geology*, George Price has an entire chapter titled, "Graveyards," in which he documents these extensive fossil burial grounds — *worldwide* — which argue for rapid burial.

No Structural Change

When one compares the creatures of the fossil record, with their living counterparts, one fact stands out clear. Though there has been some degeneracy (see above), the structural composition is the same. George Simpson cites a couple of examples: "The little sea shell *Lingula* is amazingly like its Ordovician ancestor of 400,000,000 years or so ago, and an oyster of 200,000,000 years in the past would look perfectly familiar if served in a restaurant today" (1949, 192).

A Summary

Perhaps a brief summary, highlighting the contrasts between the evolutionary "explanation" of the earth's features, and that suggested in the Bible, would be helpful. Think about the following points.

(1) The "sudden appearance" of life forms in the geologic record is better explained in terms of creation than by the "gradualistic" evolutionary view.

(2) The universal "complexity" of creatures entombed in the fossil record is more consistent with the concept of intelligent creation, than the attempt to

explain complex design by an accidental, blind, and progressive evolution.

(3) The "gaps" between the different "kinds" of plants and animals (both living and fossilized) argue more for special creation in categories of "kinds," than for gradualistic evolution.

(4) The progressive degeneration of earth's inhabitants is more in harmony with Scripture (the Edenic curse) than it is with the notion that creatures become more "fit" through the process of natural selection.

(5) The fact that ancient fossil creatures are identical in structure to their modern counterparts argues for the universal tendency of the stability of "kinds" (as stated in Genesis), rather than the transformation of life forms, as suggested by Darwinism.

(6) The massive "fossil graveyards" are more consistent with the biblical narrative (the Flood) than with the evolutionary notion of uniformitarianism.

Conclusion

A careful and honest survey of the geologic record can lead to only one conclusion. The findings of true geologic science are far more supportive of the Bible than they are the theory of evolution. This is simply beyond dispute. As Dr. Louis T. More, professor of physics at the University of Cincinnati (and an evolutionist), said a few years back in a series of lectures at Princeton University,

"The more one studies paleontology, the more certain one becomes that evolution is based upon faith alone . . ." (160).

Questions

1. Explain why some unsupported "theories" linger on longer than others.

2. Name and describe the two fundamental views of earth history.

3. What is the standard by which the "geologic timetable" has been arranged?

4. Why is the "explosion of life" in the (so-called) "earliest" stratum such a "mystery" for the evolutionist?

5. If organisms started out very "simple," and gradually evolved into "complex" forms, what would the geologist anticipate finding in the fossil record?

6. Do the major "gaps" in the fossil-laden strata better accord with the idea of *gradual* evolution, or creation according to "kinds"?

7. According to scientists who study the fossils, about what percentage of all earth's past creatures have become extinct?

8. How is the phenomenon of "degeneration" inconsistent with the evolutionary concept of "survival of the fittest"?

9. Do the vast fossil graveyards harmonize better with the catastrophism of the biblical Flood, or with the "gradualism" of Darwin's theory?

References

Darwin, Charles (6th Ed.), *The Origin of Species* (London: A.L. Burt Co.).

Dunbar, Carl (1960), *Historical Geology* (New York: John Wiley & Sons).

Free, Jack and Vos, Howard (1992), *Archaeology and Bible History* (Grand Rapids: Zondervan).

Gamow, George (1948), *Biography of the Earth - The Astonishing Life Story of Our Planet* (New York: Mentor).

Gould, Stephen J. (1977), *Natural History*, June/July.

Howard, Ted and Rifkin, Jeremy (1977), *Who Should Play God?* (New York: Dell).

Kay, Marshall and Colbert, Edwin (1965), *Straitigraphy and Life History* (New York: John Wiley and Sons).

More, Louis T. (1925), *The Dogma of Evolution* (Princeton: Princeton University Press).

Price, George M. (1913), *The Fundamentals of Geology* (Mountain View, CA: Pacific Press).

Ridley, Mark (1981), *New Scientist*, June 25.

Simpson, George G. (1944), *Tempo and Mode in Evolution* (New York: Columbia University Press).

Simpson, George G. (1949), *The Meaning of Evolution* (New Haven: Yale University Press).

Simpson, George G., Pittendrigh, C.S., Tiffany, L.H. (1957), *Life: An Introduction to Biology* (New York: Harcourt, Brace, & Co.)

Welles, Samuel P. (1979), "Fossils," *World Book Encyclopedia* (Chicago: World Book-Childcraft International, Inc.).

CHAPTER 6

THE BIBLE AND BIOLOGY

The Greek word *bios* means "life." The study of *living* things is called biology. There may be no greater mystery for science than attempting to determine what "life" is. Actually, no one knows. We know its traits or effects, but we cannot define the essence of life itself.

Identifying the Living

All material elements of the natural world may be divided into two classes, called organic and inorganic. This simply means "living" and "non-living." How does one distinguish between these two categories? There are well-established characteristics that identify when an object may be recognized as living.

(1) A living creature is able to take in food elements from the environment, combine them with oxygen, and utilize energy from these sources for the maintenance of its vital forces. Additionally, living beings excrete the waste products generated by these biological processes. This is called *metabolism.*

(2) A living being can *respond to stimuli* in the interest of its own well-being. Poke a frog with a stick and it will hop. A rock offers no response.

(3) Living systems experience *true growth* (i.e., cell multiplication). While inorganic materials may add substances to their exteriors (like a snowball rolling down

the hill), they experience no internalized growth.

(4) Living creatures are able to *reproduce* them-selves in independent organisms that replicate the original type.

(5) A living creature is capable *of autonomous movement.* An automobile moves, but it is propelled only by forces exterior to itself.

(6) Living entities are characterized by *complex organization.* The simplest living thing is far more complex than a machine manufactured by man. Notice this statement from Dr. George Simpson and his colleagues: "A modern building is certainly a complex and highly ordered structure, but its complexity cannot begin to compare with that of the living system" (262). Or note this quote from a science journal: "A pair of pliers, a chain saw or even a missile guidance system doesn't approach the lowliest parasitic worm in internal complexity. The human-made world is not nearly as intricate as the natural world" (*Science Digest,* 18). The author could have said that the man-made world is not nearly so complex as the God-made world!

The Origin of Life

In considering the issue of the origin of life, the testimony of the Bible and the beliefs of many scientists clash head-to-head. Evolutionists argue the concept of "spontaneous generation." Simpson defines the idea: "Most biologists think it probable that life did originally arise from nonliving matter by *natural* processes" (261). Unbelievably, however, on the very same page — after discussing the scientific investigations of pioneers like Francesco Redi (1626-1697) and Louis Pasteur (1822-1895) — the author confesses that by their many experiments "[i]t was demonstrated that microorganisms are carried through the air and that spontaneous generation *does not occur* in any known case" (emp. WJ). Never, in the history of science, has a known case of spontaneous generation been documented. The evidence against the accidental commencement of life is so overwhelming that scientists now acknowledge what is called "the law of biogenesis," i.e., "life comes only from life" (Simpson, 259).

On the other hand, the Scriptures clearly teach that life is the result of an act of God. Paul affirmed that God "gives to all life, and breath, and all things" (Acts 17:25; cf. Gen. 2:7; 1 Tim. 6:13). Think about the logic. If biological life is incapable of *generating itself,* since it is a fact that it exists, it must have originated from a life source of a *different* nature. That source is the "ever-living God" (cf. 1 Thes. 1:9 - the present participle asserts an eternally living being). God is really the only explanation for biological life.

Many scientists have called attention to the mathematical improbability of life being able to "jump-start" itself. Professor Conklin of Princeton compared the random origin of life to the production of an unabridged dictionary from an explosion in a print shop (62). Fred Hoyle, one of Britain's prominent men of science, likened the accidental construction of life to a vast group of blind men — 10-to-the-50th power (one followed by 50 zeros) — simultaneously solving scrambled Rubic's cubes (521-527). In other words — it won't *ever* happen!

There is another point that needs to be mentioned. Biological life is so complex that it can exist only under the most strict conditions. So far as the evidence indicates, it exists no place in the universe except on earth — where all the conditions, e.g., water, temperature, chemical components, etc., exist in just the right proportions. Some unbelieving scientists have raised this question: "Why is the earth so well fitted to life? It seems peculiar, even downright providential, as our ancestors thought it literally was" (Simpson *et al.*, 15). Some of us — those who reason logically — still think so! More and more scientists are calling the earth's environment the "anthropic" phenomenon, i.e., it appears to have been specially fashioned for man.

The Replication of Life

Exactly how are living organisms replicated? Without being technically "scientific," the Scriptures teach that in some way biological organisms reproduce "after their kind" (Gen. 1:11ff). This language is employed some ten times in Genesis 1. And while the "kinds" (Heb. *min*) mentioned in Genesis do not necessarily correspond to species, the term surely does imply certain boundaries between animal and plant groups, and it absolutely denies the common kinship of all living creatures.

Evolution, though, maintains that all living creatures have descended from an original common ancestor, a one-celled organism of some sort. It requires an incredible leap of logic to assume that just because there are creatures with one cell, and there are others with millions of cells, the former is automatically the progenitor of the later. Note this concession from Austin H. Clark, a prominent biologist who was with the Smithsonian Institution some years back:

> "It is almost invariably assumed that the animals with bodies composed of a single cell represent the primitive animals from which all others are derived. They are commonly supposed to have preceded all other animal types in their appearance. There is not the slightest basis for this assumption beyond the circumstance that in arithmetic — which is not zoology — the number one precedes the other numbers" (235-236).

Evolutionary theory has an impossible task in explaining these impassible barriers between the basic groups of biological life.

Scientists now understand something about *how* plants and animals replicate the way they do. There is a coded program called DNA. DNA stands for a chemical substance (deoxyribonucleic acid) which is in the nucleus of every living cell. This is a supermolecule that carries the genetic information necessary for the replication of the cell. It has been estimated that if the information in a single human cell were translated into English, it would constitute a library of 1,000 books of 600 pages each (Gore, 357). The DNA is a chemical code that has been compared to the information stored on the floppy disk of a computer, or in a computer microchip. Not only is the information "programmed" to replicate the entire organism, but there are elements of the program designed to produce specific features of the body, (e.g., a hand, eye, liver, etc.). As a result of the obvious "plan" within living creatures, many scientists have been forced to conclude that the DNA molecule constitutes *prima facie* evidence that an "intelligent source" was behind the planning (Thaxton, *et al.*, 211).

But there is more. DNA is only the "program" for the organism. It takes another chemical mechanism, RNA (ribonucleic acid) to actually assemble the biological data. RNA would not exist but for DNA (the latter generates the former), and DNA could produce nothing without RNA. There is a marvelous concordance between the two. This argues for design, not "accident." For a more detailed discussion, see our book, *The Human Body: Accident or Design?* (9ff).

The facts of science, combined with common sense, strongly indicate that "life" is not an accident; it was created and designed by God.

The Wonders of Living Creatures

As one studies the wide variety of living creatures that inhabit this planet, he cannot but be impressed, over and over again, that, in spite of the fact that the effect of sin (called the "bondage of corruption") has disfigured the original creation (Rom. 8:20ff), nevertheless the "finger prints" of a Creator are found everywhere. In a study as brief as this, we can only touch lightly upon such matters. But think about the following.

(1) There is an *interdependence*, and a *balance*, in nature that suggests planning. For instance, the initial forms of life upon the earth were plants. This is very

important since all animals, either directly or indirectly, depend upon plants for their food. Green leaves are the food manufacturing "plants" of the world, and they contain marvelous "chemical factories" that evidence *design* in hundreds of ways. For example, through the process known as photosynthesis, leaves are able to take carbon dioxide from the air, earth's water, and nutrients in the soil, and, in conjunction with sunlight, from them manufacture carbohydrates which supply energy for the animals that consume them. This is known as the "carbon cycle," and the process is so complex that it is not completely understood to this very day; but it certainly testifies to the wisdom of the Creator.

Have you ever thought about the reproduction ratios of various animals? Rabbits, for instance, are preyed upon by numerous predators. Accordingly, they reproduce prolifically. They can give birth to as many as nine "kits" at a time, and the gestation period is only about 30 days. Moreover, six months later the new cottontails are ready to have their own families. On the other hand elephants have few natural enemies. They normally give birth to only one offspring. The female elephant begins to bear babies when she is 14 to 15 years old, and the gestation period is almost two years. What if these reproductive features were reversed. The earth would be overrun with elephants and rabbits would have perished long ago. There is *balance* in nature.

(2) Animal *navigation* is one of the great mysteries with which advocates of evolution struggle. Ants can wander great distances from their homes, and then, taking bearings on the sun by day, or the moon by night,

invariably find their way back to their residence.

Salmon are hatched in the fresh waters of streams in the Pacific northwest. Before long they travel many miles to the ocean. When they reach sexual maturity, they head back to the same stream bed where they were spawned. En route they must make scores of choices at various forks in the rivers until they finally arrive in the very place they were hatched.

Birds migrate thousands of miles. A Baltimore oriole will leave New York in the fall for its winter vacation in South America. In May, it will return to the very same tree — after a round trip of 4,000 miles. The Arctic tern makes a 22,000 mile round trip each year — from within ten degrees of the north pole to Antarctica and back. One writer comments: "That his heart and wings are equal to [this feat] is miracle enough, but how does his tiny brain solve problems in navigation that stumped the human race for thousands of years?" (Eastman, 63).

Of what value are these bird migrations? The billions of birds that migrate control insects that otherwise would destroy tremendous areas of vegetation. One authority says: "Man could not live if the birds did not come to his assistance" (Dock, 235). How are these creatures able to accomplish these incredible journeys. Scientists are far from understanding the mechanisms of navigation. In the book, *Marvels & Mysteries of Our Animal World,* a volume that aggressively promotes evolution, a writer says that our "sonar and computers are primitive instruments compared to the devices" of some animals, e.g., the guidance system in a bat. The key question is: *How did these animals survive, over the alleged millions of years of their evolutionary history, as these guidance features were being gradually constructed?* That makes no sense. To be of any use, the system has to be perfectly operative from the start. Only the concept of purposeful design, i.e., "creation," provides a reasonable explanation for these phenomena.

(2) Most of us never think about why the world is so wonderfully colored. With us, color may be largely aesthetic; with many creatures, it's a matter of life and death. Soldiers fighting in the jungles of southeast Asia wear camouflaged garments; but, compared to creatures of the wild, man is woefully clumsy in his attempts at hiding. Who taught our animal friends how to hide?

The green frog blends with the lily pad upon which he sits, the snowshoe rabbit has brown fur in the summer, which matches the earth, but in the winter, he trades his brown coat for a white one, and is lost in the snow. If he loses a tuff of hair in the fall, the new patch that grows in will be white — in anticipation of the change a few weeks away. How did blind "mother nature" evolve the complex chemistry which so handily protects the rabbit? Many bird eggs are ingeniously designed to blend with their background, and so protect the coming offspring. A young prawn can change color completely — within a few minutes. He has a wide range of colors in his wardrobe to match his background, or the time of day.

Now here is the question no Darwinist can answer. How did these creatures slowly develop these abilities — which is the evolutionary contention — if they needed them to survive? If they could survive without them, why evolve them? If they could not survive without them, how did the species hold on while these traits were developing (by trial-and-error methodology), supposedly over eons of time? If they were designed by a master Architect, however, the problem is solved! The volume published by the Reader's Digest Association (mentioned above) admits that: "These devices, and thousands like them, are not casual happenstance" (*Marvels & Mysteries,* 256). What is their explanation? It's just a part of "nature's grand strategy" — whatever that's supposed to mean!

Conclusion

The world of biological life cannot be explained on the basis of "time" and "chance." "Mother Nature" is not a real person who could have designed and implemented the living world we see about us. One might as well contend that "Mother Goose" fashioned the planet's baffling creatures. The truth is, only the concept of an Intelligent Designer satisfies all the issues.

Questions

1. List several traits that define a "living" creature.

2. State the "law of biogenesis."

3. Why do evolutionists still cling to the theory of "spontaneous generation"?

4. What is the "anthropic" phenomenon?

5. Is the idea of creation "after its kind" in harmony with the theory that all life forms derive from a single source?

6. What is the symbol of the biological "code"?

7. What is the biblical explanation for the current "flawed" condition of the biological world?

8. Cite some examples of "balance" in the realm of biological life.

9. How does one explain the ability of certain creatures (e.g., ants) to "navigate" their travels over considerable distances. Does this ability most logically suggest "design" or "accident"?

10. Discuss the logical problem inherent in the assertion that creatures "evolved" their survival mechanisms over vast ages of time.

References

Clark, Austin H. (1930), *The New Evolution* (Baltimore: The Williams Wilkins Co.).

Conklin, Edwin (1963), *Reader's Digest,* January.

Dock, George (1964), "Why Birds Go North, " *Marvels & Mysteries of Our Animal World* (Pleasantville, NY: Reader's Digest Assoc.)

Eastman, Max (1969), "The Continuing Mystery of How Birds Navigate," *Our Amazing World of Nature* (Pleasantville, NY: Reader's Digest Assoc.).

Gore, Rick (1976), *National Geographic,* September.

Hoyle, Fred (1981), *New Scientist,* November 19.

Jackson, Wayne (1993*), The Human Body: Accident or Design?* (Stockton, CA: Courier Publications).

Science Digest (1981), April.

Simpson, George G., Pittendrigh, C.S., Tiffany, L.H. (1957), *Life: An Introduction to Biology* (New York: Harcourt, Brace).

Thaxton, Charles B., Bradley, Walter L., Olsen Roger L. (1984), *The Mystery of Life's Origin* (New York: Philosophical Library).

Chapter 7

The Bible and Anthropology

The Greeks designated man as *anthropos,* which Plato suggested was an apt description of "the being who looks up." From this word is derived "anthropology" — a study of mankind. Today, the term embraces a wide variety of ideas, including the history, distribution, physical development, and cultural peculiarities of the human species.

Modern anthropology is thoroughly dominated by the Darwinian notion that humans have evolved from a primitive life source. A textbook on this theme, currently used in many universities, is titled, *How Humans Evolved.* In the Preface, the authors assert that a consideration of evolutionary anthropology "is the key to understanding why people look and behave the way they do" (Boyd/ Silk, xviii). Biblical anthropology is light-years removed from evolutionary anthropology. In this chapter we will address several areas of interest with reference to humanity.

The Origin of Humanity

The matter of "origins" is supremely important in considering the human family. We are largely what we are, in terms of our behavior, depending upon how we view our history. If we consider ourselves to be nothing more than "naked apes," our conduct could be impacted significantly. On the other hand, if we believe that we were fashioned in the image of a holy God (Isa. 6:3; Hab. 1:13), with a religious and moral responsibility to Him, we will be inclined to live the nobler life (cf. Lev. 11:44-45; 1 Pet. 1:13-16).

Let us survey some major ideas relative to human origin.

(1) Atheistic evolution advances the notion that all forms of living creatures, including man, have evolved by strictly natural processes from a primitive spark of life that was spontaneously generated. This viewpoint is wholly philosophical, with no genuine scientific basis. Note: (a) The evolutionary scenario cannot explain the origin of matter. So far as the evidence is concerned, matter is not eternal, nor does it have the ability to create itself. (b) Darwinism provides no evidence that life could have generated itself (see the chapter on Biology). (c) Furthermore, the *necessary mechanisms* for developing the vast world of living creatures from an original, one-cell organism simply do not exist.

The two commonly-postulated explanations for the molecule-to-man hypothesis are *random genetic mutations* and *natural selection*. Neither is a sufficient cause for what is observed in the world today.

(a) *Genetic mutations* (alterations of genetic material) rarely occur, and they are almost always debilitating (frequently lethal). One can hardly use a *regressive* process to explain a phenomenon that allegedly is *progressive*. Even the late Dr. George Simpson conceded that if one assumed an effective breeding population of 100 million individuals, and they could produce a new generation each day, the likelihood of obtaining good evolutionary results from mutations could be expected only once in about 274 billion years (96). Evolutionists estimate the age of the earth at only about 5 billion years!

(b) *Natural selection* is currently one of the most disputed points of evolution doctrine, even among the devotees of Darwinism. It functions as a filtering process, by which the more unfit are eliminated, but it cannot produce organisms more complex than the original. C.H. Waddington, who served as Professor of Animal Genetics at Edinburgh University, described the notion that evolution can be explained, on the basis of "natural selection," as a "lunatic sort of logic," and he, as an evolutionist, opined: "I think we should be able to do better" (38).

(2) There are those who lie under the spell of evolutionary dogma, yet, they acknowledge that evolution, as a purely naturalistic system, is inadequate to explain the biological world. Hence, they feel obligated to introduce "God" into the equation as a cure-all for the problems of that ideology. It is thus argued that God started life initially, and He has guided the evolutionary process at various junctures subsequently. This concept is known as "theistic evolution." Theistic evolution resorts to manipulating the biblical text (e.g., creating a gap of billions of years between Genesis 1:1 and 1:2, viewing the "days" of the initial week as long periods of time — contra Exodus 20:11, rearranging the order of days in the creation week, etc.). In this interpretative scheme, Adam and Eve become mere "symbols," and Jesus and His apostles are discredited for their literal approach to Genesis (cf. Mt. 19:4; Rom. 5:15; 2 Cor. 11:3; 1 Tim. 2:13-14).

(3) Finally, there is the biblical view; it is pure and uncluttered by ancient myth (such as characterized the Babylonian creation epic). The entire creation occurred by divine fiat during a period of six, literal days. The Scriptures provide no endorsement to the constantly-being-revised evolutionary scheme. W.F. Albright, a world-famous archaeologist, and certainly no conservative scholar, wrote:

> "The account of Creation which we find in chapter 1 [of Genesis] is unique in ancient literature. It undoubtedly reflects an advanced monotheistic point of view, with a sequence of creative phases which is so rational that modern science cannot improve on it, given the same language and the same range of ideas in which to state its conclusions. In fact, modern scientific cosmogonies show such a disconcerting tendency to be short-lived that it may be seriously doubted whether science has yet caught up with the Biblical story" (135).

The Uniqueness of Mankind

No consideration of anthropology can be balanced that does not treat the unique qualities of man — those traits that distance him from the brute creation beneath him. While modern anthropologists argue that man is but "a naked ape self-named *Homo sapiens*" (Morris, 9), the real evidence is quite against that idea. In fact, as atheist Julian Huxley begrudgingly acknowledges, "the man-animal gap [is] broadening," and he thinks the cause may be the "increase of knowledge and the extension of scientific analysis" (2-3).

(1) There are numerous important *physical* distinc-

tions between humans and apes. We can note but a few of these: the axis of the human head is positioned to accommodate upright walking; the ape's feet are designed for grasping; most of man's brain development is post-birth; ape arms are fashioned longer to accommodate tree-swinging; there are vastly different mating patterns between humans and apes, etc.

It is commonly claimed that there is fossil evidence demonstrating man's apish ancestry. In 1974 a few skeleton fragments were found in Ethiopia that were subsequently named, "Lucy." But the Lucy-human connection is highly disputed. William Fix (no creationist), in his book, *The Bone Peddlers*, has an entire chapter called, "The Lucy Caper." The bone fragments for "Lucy" were gathered from several places (at different depths); there is no evidence that they represent anything other than animal bones (Pitman, 249). Some evolutionists even argue there is reason to believe (based upon footprints found in hardened volcanic ash in Tanzania, Africa) that true human beings pre-dated "Lucy" considerably (Robbins, 452), and that she was not, therefore, a creature on-the-way to becoming a human. There is no fossil evidence of a half-ape, half-human creature, in spite of outrageous claims to the contrary.

(2) There are many psychological differences that separate humans from the ape-kind. Humans possess self-awareness and the ability to reflect upon their history. Man plans for the future, ever longing for improvement. Human beings have a sense of the aesthetic. No monkey admires a sunset or composes a sympathy. Mankind accumulates knowledge over the ages; today's ape is

as "dumb" as one of thirty centuries past. Humans have a spiritual urge; no chimp does. There is a vast chasm between these two inhabitants of earth.

The Antiquity of Man

Evolutionary chronology alleges that the universe is approximately 20 billion years old. Supposedly, the earth was born about 5 billion years ago. It is contended that biological life spontaneously arose some 2-3 billion years in the past. Finally, it is suggested that true man, as a Johnny-come-lately, developed approximately 2-3 million years back in history.

The motive for this exaggerated chronology is the need for time, so that evolution has the opportunity to occur. "Time is in fact the hero of the plot," confessed Dr. George Wald (48). Again, however, the evidence has been seriously misrepresented by those whose aim it is to dismiss God. As Huxley affirmed, "God is no longer a useful hypothesis" (281). But the facts are these.

(1) There is no fail-safe method for determining the age of the earth or man, based upon the "decay" methods, e.g. uranium-to-lead, or carbon 14. All such dating methods are based upon assumptions.

For example in the uranium-lead process (wherein uranium decays, ultimately becoming lead): (a) It must be assumed that one's sample did not contain a deposit of lead already; (b) it must be assumed that the decay rate has always remained constant; and, (c) it must be assumed that during the decay process there has been no contamination from extraneous sources. Each of these assumptions is highly questionable, and there is considerable evidence that neuters the force of the long-age contention.

For further study, see our book, *Creation, Evolution, and the Age of the Earth.*

(2) The notion that man has been on earth for more than a million years is at variance with biblical data. From the present back to the time of Abraham is only about 4,000 years. According to Jesus' genealogical record in Luke 3, there are but twenty generations between Abraham and Adam, the first man (1 Cor. 15:45), which could only encompass a relatively brief span of time. Even if one allowed for minor gaps in the Messianic genealogy (cf. Gen. 11:12; Lk. 3:36), there is no way a million or so years can be squeezed into that record. If the genealogical list does not contain lineage proximity, it is a meaningless assemblage of words.

Furthermore, Jesus *Himself* placed man back at the very "beginning of the creation" (Mk. 10:6). It is impossible to accept the Lord's statement, and, at the same time, contend that the universe commenced 20 billion years ago, while man arrived only a couple of million years back in history.

The only reasonable approach to the Bible is to view the entire creation as a relatively recent event. And the truth of the matter is, there is no hard-core scientific evidence that contradicts this view.

The Nature of Man

The psalmist pondered: "What is man, that thou art mindful of him?" (Psa. 8:4). The atheist contends that man consists of nothing but matter. Who can really believe such a bizarre philosophy? Do we treat a human being as we would a piece of wood, or even a dog? Why do we eat cattle but not men? Why are there different rules for human conduct versus that for animals? Do we prosecute and incarcerate a dog for stealing a bone?

The Scriptures unequivocally declare that man is more than material substance. Rather, he has been made in the very "image" of God (Gen. 1:26), who does not consist of flesh and blood (Mt. 16:17). Humans must, therefore, possess something beyond the physical. It is called "soul" or "spirit." Daniel was grieved in his "spirit," which was within his body (Dan. 7:15). The Lord warned that God is able to punish both "body and soul" (Mt. 10:28). The spirit is the "knowing," "feeling" part of man (1 Cor. 2:11; 16:18). It is that which sometimes is called "conscience," and which will survive the death of the body (2 Cor. 5:1ff; Rev. 6:9ff). See the following chapters on "Psychology," and also "The Amazing Human Mind."

The Purpose of Man

It is a tragic character indeed who does not recognize his purpose for being on this globe. David Hume, the Scottish philosopher who did so much to oppose Christianity, in his famous *Treatise of Human Nature*, wrote: "Where am I, or what? From what causes do

I derive my existence, and to what condition shall I return? . . . I am confounded with all these questions, and begin to fancy myself in the most deplorable condition imaginable, envisioned with the deepest darkness, and utterly deprived of the use of every member and faculty" (quoted by Smith, 553).

Humanity was made to glorify God (Isa. 43:7); this is not because the Creator needs that adulation (Acts 17:25), rather it is because our greatest happiness lies in serving God. As Mary, mother of the Lord, once expressed it: "My soul doth magnify the Lord, and my spirit hath rejoiced in God my Savior" (Lk. 1:46). Thus, the whole duty of man is to reverence his Maker and keep His commandments (Eccl. 12:13). The person who neglects to serve the Creator has wasted his life.

The Fall and Redemption of Man

No balanced discussion of anthropology would be complete without mention of the greatest human tragedy of all — apostasy from God. Through willful sin, human beings become estranged from their Creator (Isa. 59:1-2), hence, are said to be spiritually "dead" (Eph. 2:1ff). Because of His holy nature (Hab. 1:13), God could not merely overlook this matter, lest His own integrity be compromised. The options for dealing with this problem obviously were limited. It was either let humanity remain lost — forever isolated from the blessings of association with Deity — or else, provide a means of redemption for the fallen race. How was this sad circumstance to be remedied? How could God remain just, and yet justify wayward man?

Because of His great love (1 Jn. 4:8; Jn. 3:16), the Father offered His Son, Jesus Christ, as an atoning sacrifice for human sin (see Rom. 3:21-26). The prophets had previewed it (Isa. 53), and the Gospel writers detail its fulfillment. When we, in an obedience — generated by faith — submit to His will, pardon can be ours (Heb. 5:8-9; Acts 2:38; 22:16). Thanks be to God for His unspeakable gift (2 Cor. 9:15).

The Destiny of Man

Finally, what is the *ultimate* human reality? After the body has eroded back to the dust of the earth, what then? Shall we sob, as did the skeptical Madame Marie Curie, when she reflected upon the burial of her beloved husband (who was tragically killed), "it is the end of everything, everything, everything" (Curie, 249).

Logic demands that beyond the grave there is either "nothing" or "something." If death is the end of human existence, then life is a meaningless riddle, and it matters not how one lives. If there is something beyond death, surely it is either "good" or "bad" — or both. If it is all good, or all bad, what difference does conduct in this life make? If one's destiny, however, is determined by the manner of his life, and whether such is in response to the will of God, it behooves any thinking person to be serious about eternity. The Scriptures teach that the destiny of humanity will be either *with* God, or *without* him (Mt. 25:31ff). The latter is simply too horrible to contemplate.

Conclusion

Man is the only creature on earth who is interested in his past, his purpose, and his future. Surely this should be an index into his soul. The wise person will pursue the answers to these queries with all diligence.

Questions

1. Discuss the relationship between the view one entertains of his origin, and his manner of living.

2. List three main issues relative to "origins" that evolution cannot address.

3. Name the two alleged "mechanisms" of the evolutionary process.

4. Why are "genetic mutations" inadequate to explain the evolutionary theory?

5. What is the limitation of the "natural selection" process?

6. Define "theistic evolution," and cite some of the compromising manipulations of the biblical record which attempt to accommodate this viewpoint.

7. List several traits (physical and/or psychological) that distinguish humans from apes.

8. Why is "time" the "hero of the plot" in the doctrine of evolution?

9. List three assumptions in the "decay" dating techniques.

10. Can Jesus' statement in Mark 10:6 be harmonized with evolutionary chronology? Explain.

11. Contrast the "purpose" of mankind, as viewed from the creationist and evolutionary standpoints.

12. If man has "risen," rather than "fallen," how does this relate to the plan of redemption?

References

Albright, W.F. (1948), "The Old Testament and Archaeology," *Old Testament Commentary*, H.C. Alleman and E.E. Flack, Eds. (Philadelphia: Muhlenberg Press).

Boyd, Robert and Silk, Joan (1997), *How Humans Evolved* (New York: W.W. Norton & Co.).

Curie, Eve (1937), *Madame Curie: A Biography* (Garden City, NY: Doubleday).

Fix, William (1984), *The Bone Peddlers* (New York: Macmillan).

Huxley, Julian (1941), *The Uniqueness of Man* (London: Chatto & Windus).

Morris, Desmond (1967), *The Naked Ape* (New York: McGraw-Hill).

Pitman, Michael (1984), *Adam and Evolution* (London: Rider & Co.).

Robbins, Louise (1979), quoted in *National Geographic*, April.

Simpson, George G. (1953), *The Major Features of Evolution* (New York: Columbia University Press).

Smith, Wilbur (1945), *Therefore Stand* (Boston: W.A. Wilde Co.).

Wald, George (1954), "The Origin of Life," *Scientific American*, August.

Waddington, C.H. (1961), "Evolution," *Science Today - Talks By Fifteen Outstanding Scientists* (New York: Criterion Books).

CHAPTER 8

THE BIBLE AND ANATOMY-PHYSIOLOGY

A thousand years before the birth of Jesus, David, exclaimed to the God he so loved: "I will give thanks unto you; for I am fearfully and wonderfully made: Wonderful are your works, and that my soul knows right well" (Psa. 139:14). Far in advance of our sophisticated knowledge of anatomy and physiology, Israel's great king proclaimed the human body as an evidence for the existence of Jehovah. His creation of "man" (human kind) from the dust of the earth inspires both wonder and reverence in people who think beyond the superficial.

Centuries later Paul would write to the church at Corinth, encouraging them toward congregational unity. As an analogy, he employed the example of the harmonious operation of the various components of the human body, affirming: "But now hath God set each one of them in the body, even as it pleased him" (1 Cor. 12:18). The verb "set" is interesting. It is frequently used of the Lord's creative activity. He "set" the stars in their places (Gen. 1:17), and "set" the bounds that hold back the sea (Job 38:10).

Is the human body a "freak" accident of nature, or has it been purposefully designed. That is the question upon which this study will focus. Where does the evidence point? Anatomy is the study of the *structure* of the various parts of the human body; physiology is the investigation of the *action* of those components.

Organization

The human body is a mini-universe, amazingly constructed with precise organization. Dr. Simpson of Harvard, a leading proponent of evolution, described the body "the most highly endowed organization of matter that has yet appeared on the earth" (293). The student hardly needs to be reminded that things, left to themselves in nature, tend toward *dis*organization. The organization of our bodies, therefore, argues for something more than mere "nature" behind the scenes.

The body has been organized on four levels. First, there is the *cell* — the smallest unit of life. It is a microscopic galaxy of organized activity. Cells come in different types, e.g., blood cells, nerve cells, etc.

Second, cells of the same sort operate in concert; their effort is called a *tissue,* and there are varieties of tissues (e.g., skin, muscle, etc.).

Third, a cooperative group of tissues constitute an *organ.* Organs (e.g., the liver, heart, etc.) accomplish different functions within the body.

Fourth, organs that work together are called a *system* (e.g., the nervous system, the digestive system, etc.). It is generally recognized that there are ten of these systems operating in concert to facilitate the activity of our marvelous bodies.

Surely only the most obtuse can fail to see that there is design in this organization. In fact, Dr. William Beck, who was associated with Harvard for years — and a thorough-going evolutionist — wrote a book titled, *Human Design.* Since there is a fundamental principle of logic which states: "Where there is design, there must be a designer," one is bound to conclude that man's body is the product of intelligent design (God), not random chance.

Cells

It is estimated that there are some 100 trillion cells in the human body (Beck, 189). On average, each of them is less than 1/1000th of an inch in length. Yet they are astoundingly complicated. The cell is covered with a membrane that has an "uncanny molecular memory" (Borek, 5), that knows just what to let in and let out. Within the membrane is a watery substance called cytoplasm, which is bustling with activity. There are miniature power plants, transportation systems, sewage operations, protective systems, etc.

One evolutionary source confesses that no man-made system "however ingenious and efficient" can match "the functions of this single unit of life, too small to be seen with the unaided eye" (Miller/Goode, 162).

A Systematized Operation

The Basic Dictionary of Science defines a system as "any group of things or parts working together to give a united effect . . . all the different structures *specially designed* to take part in one complex operation or having one purpose . . ." (469; emp. added). The author said more than he intended. If the systems of the body are "specially designed," they must have had a designer! The "law of design" demands this. Let us meditate upon some of the body's intriguing systems. (For further study, see our book, *The Human Body - Accident or Design?*.)

(1) *The Skin System* - The skin is the largest organ of the body, and it is a very busy place. "A piece of skin about the size of a quarter contains 1 yard of blood vessels, 4 yards of nerves, 25 nerve ends, 100 sweat glands, and more than 3 million cells" (Youmans, 17:404d). The skin serves several vital purposes: (a) It is a protective covering; (b) It holds the fluids within the body; (c) It shields the interior parts of the body from harmful rays of the sun; (d) Its nerves are warning sensors for cold, heat, pain, etc. (e) The sweat glands cool the body; (f) Oil glands provide lubrication; (g) And just think; when the skin gets cut, it repairs itself. No house constructed by man has the ability to patch its own roof!

(2) *The Skeleton System* - The average adult has 206 bones. They serve the body in a variety of crucial ways. (a) Some form the inner framework, like wall studs in a house. (b) Others provide a protective covering (e.g., the skull). (c) They function as levers, in conjunction with certain muscles (like those in the arms and legs). (d) Bones serve a metabolic purpose as well. Minerals (like calcium and phosphorus) are manufactured in the bones, and certain blood cells arise in the bone marrow.

(3) *The Muscle System* - The human body has more than 600 muscles. They have been described as the body's "engines." Can an engine develop by accident? Dr. John Lenihan, an evolutionist, confesses that the human body "is vastly more complicated than any man-made engine" (152). Muscles are wonderfully designed. Some, like the heart, operate automatically. One doesn't even

have to think about them. Others, like the biceps in the arm, are under the control of a person's will. Some function both voluntarily and involuntarily. You may "blink" your eyes purposefully, or just forget about it, and they'll do the work "automatically" for you.

(4) *The Digestive System* - The average person will consume 40 tons of food during a lifetime. The body has been marvelously fashioned to process the food, using it to rebuild worn-out cells and to supply energy for work and play. Digestion begins the moment food is in the mouth; chemicals within one's saliva commence the process. Digestion in the stomach is a remarkable phenomenon. Note this comment from two evolutionists: "We would have to boil our food in strong acids at 212 degrees Fahrenheit to do with cookery what the stomach and intestines do at the body's normal temperature of 98.6 degrees" (Miller & Goode, 108). And isn't it amazing that the stomach, made of flesh, does not digest itself while it is digesting your steak?! The fact is, the lining of the stomach is rebuilt every three days.

(5) *The Circulatory System* - How does the food you eat get to the various parts of your body, in order to nourish them? By means of the circulatory system, i.e., the heart and blood vessels. The heart is a pump with a built-in motor. This involuntary muscle beats about 100,000 times a day, pumping some 1,800 gallons of blood through its chambers. Miller & Goode acknowledge that "it is hard to imagine a better job of engineering" (68) — though they believe that blind "Mother Nature" was the engineer! The blood is pumped through an astounding pipeline system (the arteries, veins, and

capillaries), which, if tied end-to-end, would stretch out for some 60,000 to 100,000 miles. Does anyone believe that the underground pipeline system of San Francisco contrived itself? Only disciples of Darwin are so credulous.

(6) *The Nervous System* - The nervous system is the communication center of the body. It consists of the brain (the body's computer), along with the spinal cord, and the nerves — which spread out all over the body, carrying messages (at some 450 feet per second — more than 300 m.p.h.) to and from the brain. Dr. John Pfeiffer, one of the world's foremost experts on the nervous system, called it "the most elaborate communications system ever devised" (4). Devised? Who devised it?

The brain is a vast library of information. Atheist Carl Sagan estimated that the brain's storage capacity is the equivalent of a library of 20 million volumes. It would take a bookshelf stretching from San Francisco, California to Portland, Oregon to house the data stored in man's brain. Is it possible to believe that this kind of library just happened?

The *Encyclopedia Britannica* says that "problem solving by a human brain exceeds by far the capacity of the most powerful computer" (2:189). And space fails us to tell of the brilliant functions of the eyes, ears, nose, tongue, etc. But we have discussed all this, and more, in our book dealing with the body.

(7) *The Reproductive System* - John Lenihan has been described as "one of the world's most eminent bioengineers." His fascinating book, *Human Engineering — The Body Re-Examined*, is a study of the engineering tech-

niques employed in the design of the body. He considers each of the body's systems and notes the analogies between these and the machines man has built, concluding that the former are far superior. When he comes to the reproductive system, however, he becomes strangely silent. Why? Because, as he explains, "biological replication" has no modern counterpart in man-made machinery.

Man cannot build a machine that is able to reproduce itself. But God did! Miller and Goode stood in awe of the reproductive system, calling it "almost too fantastic to believe." No, what is "too fantastic to believe," is that it happened purely by chance — as the advocates of evolution assert!

The process of sexual reproduction is much too technical to be discussed in this brief section. It is sufficient to say that dozens of activities must operate precisely in concert for it to be operative. If one part fails, the system fails, and the species comes to an end. The mathematical odds of this system developing fortuitously are astronomical beyond belief — which means *never*.

I once sat in a philosophy class and heard the professor discuss this matter of evolution and "odds." He suggested that *anything* is *possible*. He speculated that one might hold a shotgun six inches from the face of a potential victim, and discharge the weapon. He then claimed that it would be "mathematically possible" that none of the shot would strike the target! He did not volunteer, of course, to demonstrate his theory.

The Great Symphony

Each system of the human body is an absolute wonder itself. Even more astounding is how they work together in such beautiful harmony — like a grand symphony orchestrated by a master composer. Indeed, there was a Master Composer! "I will give thanks unto you; for I am fearfully and wonderfully made" (Psa. 139:14).

Think about this. If it were not for the digestive system, we could not process our food and thus have the nourishment we need. But it would scarcely be of any value for food to be digested if there was no way for it to reach the remote parts of the body, hence the need for the circulatory system. But the circulatory system could not function without directions from the nervous system; these components must be synchronized. But the nervous system could not operate if not for the elements it receives that are manufactured in the bones.

This is but a minute sampling of the sort of integration that the "galaxy" of the body must have. This positively shows that the various constituents of the human body could not have developed in piece-meal fashion, over vast ages of time. The system had to be fully operational at the very beginning. What powerful testimony this is to the fact that our bodies are masterpieces of design.

Are There Flaws?

Atheists argue, however, that if the human body had been designed by a perfect God, there would be no flaws in it. Since there are problems, they allege, this negates our argument of divine design.

Richard Dawkins, an atheist in England, has written a book titled, *The Blind Watchmaker*. Therein he argues that our eyes have been "wired backwards," though he concedes that the eyes work wonderfully well anyhow. He says he doesn't know what to make of "this strange state of affairs" (96). More recently, though, Dr. Michael Denton, Senior Research Fellow in Human Molecular Genetics, at the University of Otago, Dunedin, New Zealand, has taken Dawkins to the proverbial "woodshed." Denton has argued that this very "wired backwards" phenomenon appears to reflect brilliant planning which solves several problems related to sight. Denton specifically says that the feature "is evidence for design and foresight in nature rather than evidence of chance" (14-17). Incidentally, Denton does not classify himself as a "creationist." For a more complete discussion of this matter, see (Jackson, 1999, 15).

Several factors must be kept in mind when one begins to consider "flaws" or weaknesses in the human body. (1) There are some features of the body which simply may not be understood. Until relatively recent times, the appendix was in this category. There are still many mysteries of the body that we've not yet fathomed. (2) The Bible plainly teaches that humanity, due to the effects of sin, has suffered a degenerative process (Rom. 5:12; 8:18ff). We are not what we used to be — either as individuals or as a species. (3) A machine may evince design, even though some of its parts are broken. A watch demands a watch-maker, even if it no longer keeps the time as accurately as it once did.

Conclusion

When all of the data in the fields of anatomy and physiology are analyzed, it is quite evident that the human body is a masterpiece of design. Dr. Harrell Dodson, Jr., for many years Clinical Professor of Surgery at the University of Oklahoma College of Medicine, has said that the "special functions of the human body . . . would be impossible to develop by evolution from another form of life" (Jackson, 1993, "Foreword"). A book recently published by the Reader's Digest Association, known for the promotion of Darwinism, forthrightly admits:

> "When you come right down to it, the most incredible *creation* in the universe is you . . . The body is a structural masterpiece more amazing than science fiction" (Guinness, 5; emp. WJ).

Right! And it took a *Creator* to produce that creation; and a *Master* to produce that masterpiece!

Questions

1. Discuss David and Paul's assessment of the human body (Psa. 139:14; 1 Cor. 12:18).

2. Discuss the "organizational" tendency in nature, versus the highly organized structures of the human body. Does it seem reasonable that "nature" could have designed the body?

3. Name the four organizational levels of the body.

4. How does a "system" argue for design? What is "the law of design"?

5. Name as many of the body's systems as you can.

6. List several functions of the bones.

7. Name some "voluntary" muscles, some "involuntary" muscles, and some that are both.

8. What are some material analogies that illustrate the nervous system in general and the brain in particular?

9. Cite some examples of the mutual dependency of the body's various systems.

10. How does the Bible-believer account for some of the "apparent flaws" in the human body?

References

Beck, William S. (1971), *Human Design* (New York: Harcourt, Brace, Jovanovich).

Borek, Ernest (1973), *The Sculpture of Life* (New York: Columbia University Press).

Dawkins, Richard (1986), *The Blind Watchmaker* (New York: W.W. Norton & Co,).

Denton, Michael (1999), "The Inverted Retina: Maladaptation or Pre-adaptation?," *Origins & Design*, Winter.

Encyclopedia Britannica (1989), "Bionics," (Chicago: Encyclopedia Britannica, Inc.).

Guinness, Alma, Ed. (1987), *ABC's of The Human Body* (Pleasantville, NY: Reader's Digest Association).

Jackson, Wayne (1993*), The Human Body: Accident or Design?* (Stockton, CA: Courier Publications).

Jackson, Wayne (1999), "The 'Eye' Of The Evolutionary Storm, *Christian Courier,* August.

Lenihan, John (1974), *Human Engineering* (New York: George Braziller, Inc.).

Miller, Benjamin and Goode, Ruth (1960), *Man and His Body* (New York: Simon & Schuster).

Simpson, George G. (1949), *The Meaning of Evolution* (New Haven: Yale University Press).

Youmans, W.B. (1979), *World Book Encyclopedia* (Chicago: World Book-Childcraft International).

CHAPTER 9

THE AMAZING HUMAN MIND

In previous chapters, we have discussed the relationship of the Bible to some of the physical sciences. Now, at least for a while, we will move into a broader area of "science" — one more abstract — which deals with the "mind" of man.

Atheism contends that man is wholly mortal; he has no "spirit" essence. But that view is not supported by the best evidence. There is more to the human being than flesh, bone, and blood. If, then, we are in a genuine quest for "knowledge" about the "science" of mankind, the "mental" or "spiritual" side of our make-up must be addressed.

The Genesis record affirms that humanity was made in the "image" of God (1:26-27). That this has no reference to a *physical* image is apparent from the fact that God is not a physical being. As to His nature, He is spirit (Jn. 4:24), and spirit is of an entirely different "essence" than flesh, bones, and blood (Lk. 24:39; Mt. 16:17; cf. Hos. 11:9). Man's reflection of Jehovah's "image," therefore, must have to do with another aspect of His makeup. Obviously, it is the human mind (soul, spirit) that has been fashioned in the divine likeness.

Man's "mind" is that part of him which has self-awareness, which contemplates, reflects, purposes, understands, and evaluates. "Mind" has to do with our intellect and emotions. It is an interesting fact that some eighteen different words in the Greek New Testament are employed to depict different aspects of the human mind. Human beings have "mind;" animals do not.

The Amazing Mind

Think about your mind for a moment. (And we humans are the only ones who ever ponder our minds. The ape doesn't!) The "mind" operates through the brain, as an instrument. The brain houses the mind. A corpse has a brain, but no mind. So far as one's earthly existence is concerned, there is a close relationship between the brain and the mind. We must, therefore, reflect again upon some of the wonders of the human brain.

Your brain, according to the late Isaac Asimov (an atheist), is "the most complex and orderly arrangement of matter in the universe" (10). Dr. Robert Jastrow (an agnostic) authored a book titled, *The Enchanted Loom: Mind in the Universe.* In this volume he compared the memory capacity of the human brain to a computer. He suggested that if scientists were to construct a computer comparable to the human brain, it would require half the electrical output of Grand Coulee Dam to operate it, take most of the Empire State Building to house it, and would cost $10 billion to build. Still, it "would be only a clumsy imitation of the human brain" (142-43).

In his book, *Broca's Brain*, noted atheist Carl Sagan compared the human brain to a vast library containing some twenty million volumes, comparable to the world's largest libraries (275). These skeptics had one thing in common — they each believed the marvelous mind of man is but an evolutionary accident, a freak occurrence in nature. Prominent evolutionist Loren Eiseley described the matter in the following language:

> "For three billion years, until an ageless watcher might have turned away in weariness, nothing had moved but the slime and its creations. In all that prehuman world there had been no animal capable of looking back or forward. No living creature had wept above another's grave. There had been nothing to comprehend the whole . . . . At the end of that time there occurred a small soundless explosion . . . in a little packet of gray matter that quite suddenly appears to have begun to multiply in the thick-walled cranium of a ground dwelling ape" (quoted by Miller & Goode, 271).

If anyone spun that sort of "yarn" (the "little bang" theory) in attempting to explain the origin of the computer, he would be laughed out of court. But in the halls of "evolutionary science," anything can pass muster.

The Dimensions of Memory

No one really has plumbed the depths of the capability and the capacity of the amazing human mind. One scholar, who has made a special study of the brain, says:

> "The dimensions of human memory have never been measured, but rough estimates indicate the general capacity of the brain's storehouses . . . . During your lifetime you can store about ten times more information than is contained in the nine million volumes of the Library of Congress" (Pfeiffer, 85).

It has been said that if one memorized material twenty-four hours a day for his entire life, he would not exhaust the phenomenal storage reservoir of the mind. History has provided us with some remarkable examples of the mind's prowess. The following unusual cases are cited from Webster's chapter, "The Mystery of Memory" (93-106).

Wolfgang Mozart once memorized an entire musical score after hearing it only once; later, he precisely reproduced it on paper. A man named Robert H. Nutt, from North Carolina, could be introduced successively to 200 people and then walk among them, calling each by name.

Chess is a particularly complex game. It is said that the first ten moves by each player in a chess match can be made in more than 169,500,000,000,000, 000,000,000,000,000 different moves. In 1941, Gideon Shahlberg played 400 games simultaneously; after a grueling 36-hour contest, he had 364 wins, 14 ties, and 22 losses. Salo Finkelstein was a "human calculator." He could add columns of four figures faster than could be done on an adding machine.

The Conscious and Subconscious

Most of the things we do on a given day we do not even consciously think about. When you get up in the morning, you give little, if any, concentration to brushing your teeth, shaving, or applying makeup. Most of the time when we are driving our automobiles, we are doing *automatically* several activities at the same time. Some have said that a person really concentrates on what he is doing about one minute out of each hour; most things we do simply by rote memory.

The mind seems to have the strange and unique ability of being able to take in vast stores of information, some of which is assembled for ready use, but much of which is stored on "back shelves" to be used later if needed. Authorities suggest that most of that which invades our brain via the senses is "forgotten" (some say as much as 90%). It has been shown, however, that much of what we think we've forgotten, actually is recorded somewhere in the inner recesses of the mind.

As virtually everyone knows, there are experiences (memories) stored away in the mind, of which we have not been conscious for decades. How many times has a smell, a song, or some scene triggered a long-forgotten memory from childhood. If asked, most of us could recall what "Little Miss Muffit" sat on, and what "Jack Sprat" could not eat, though we've not heard these rhymes in eons! A scientist at the University of Vermont put several adult subjects under hypnosis. When these people were asked on what day of the week certain childhood birthdays or Christmases fell, they could clearly recall them. Electrical stimulation of the brain can also cause certain latent memories, seemingly long forgotten, to emerge. Two evolutionists have unwittingly given tribute to this element of divine creation: "There is nothing in the world, natural or man-made, that matches the human memory" (Miller & Goode, 294).

The Blessing of Forgetting

Perhaps we don't think about it as much, but the ability to "forget" is as great a blessing as "remembering." Suppose that everything you ever had learned was right in the forefront of your attention. You simply would not be able to function under that condition. What if the mechanic was forced to think about everything he knew about automobiles each time he saw a car? What if, each time you did a math problem, every step of learning mathematics came roaring back into your consciousness? Many of the facts and concepts recorded in the brain, therefore, are sort of "filed away" because we do not need them immediately; more urgent matters solicit our attention. The mind has a wonderful "sorting" mechanism.

Too, think of the emotional benefits of being able to forget. What would it be like if each physical pain (and pain is a brain sensation), or each heartache, remained as vivid as the moment you first experienced it? One could not be sane under such a circumstance. While we extol the virtue of memory, we must not forget to be thankful that we can forget!

Spiritual Lessons

The consultation of a Bible concordance will reveal that there are numerous sacred passages which mention remembering, or its equivalent — not forgetting. Let us consider some of these (and this by no means exhausts the list).

(1) Human beings are admonished to remember God. We are to remember that He is our Creator (Eccl.

12:1), and that He has gloriously manifested Himself in a myriad of ways. "Seek Jehovah and his strength; seek his face evermore. Remember his marvelous works that he has done, his wonders and the judgments of his mouth" (Psa. 105:4-5).

(2) Truly remembering God means humbly submitting to His plan for your life. Moses wrote: "Beware lest you forget Jehovah your God, in not keeping his commandments, and his ordinances, and his statutes, which I command you this day" (Dt. 8:11). This corresponds with a blunt New Testament warning: "He who says, I know him [God], and keeps not his commandments, is a liar, and the truth is not in him" (1 Jn. 2:4).

(3) There is a standard of conduct that the Lord expects even of nations. "Righteousness exalts a nation; but sin is a reproach to any people" (Prov. 14:34). When a nation abandons principles of justice, God will judge it. "The wicked shall be turned back unto Sheol, even all the nations that forget God" (Psa. 9:17). When arrogant nations forget God, He remembers them! Of the vile kingdom of Israel, a prophet, speaking for Jehovah, said: "And they consider not in their hearts that I remember all their wickedness . . ." (Hos. 7:2). [Note: The Creator's dealings with humans are frequently described figuratively, in terms of divine "forgetting" and "remembering." This is a form of "anthropomorphism," symbolically depicting deity in human terms.]

(4) It has been said that those who do not remember the lessons (mistakes) of history are destined to repeat them. That surely is why the Lord repeatedly admonished Israel to reflect back on how He had delivered them

when they were obedient to His will. When the children of Israel left the land of bondage, Moses enjoined:

> "Remember this day, in which you came out from Egypt, out of the house of bondage; for by strength of hand Jehovah brought you out from this place . . ." (Ex. 13:3).

The apostle Peter dealt with a group of materialistic mockers who denied that Christ would return to judge the world. Their argument was this: The natural order of things has been uninterrupted for centuries. Thus, one may assume that no judgment is forthcoming. To this shallow conclusion the apostle responded: "For this they wilfully forget [sometimes it's called "suppression"!] . . . ." He then cites the case of the universal flood in Noah's day (2 Pet. 3:5ff).

(5) Jeremiah, on behalf of the Lord, once inquired of rebellious Judah: "Can a virgin forget her ornaments, or a bride her attire? Yet my people have forgotten me days without number" (Jer. 2:32). It is a realistic truth that we are inclined to remember those things for which we have a genuine interest. Some can remember countless baseball statistics, but they cannot remember the names of the books of the Bible or the simple components of the plan of redemption.

(6) The Bible indicates that memory will be a part of the after-death experience. When the rich man of Luke 16:19ff passed from the scenes of this earth, he pled for relief from his torment. He was told, however: "Son, remember that in your lifetime . . ." (25). In the altar vision of Revelation 6, John heard the martyrs inquiring

regarding the fate of their earthly brethren, recalling their unjust suffering. Earth's events had not fled their memories.

(7) Those who have surrendered to the conditions of the "new birth" (Jn. 3:3-5), and thus have refreshed their souls in the blessings of the "in Christ" relationship, have to learn to forget some things that are behind them. Paul the apostle wrote: ". . . forgetting the things which are behind, and stretching forward to the things which are before, I press on toward the goal unto the prize of the high calling of God in Christ Jesus" (Phil. 3:13-14). We must forget past accomplishments (cf. 3:7-8; cf. Ezek. 18:24) and live each day vigorously in the service of the Lord. We should attempt to forget the blunders we have made — God has (Jer. 31:34).

(8) Some, who once served the Savior with dedication, have lapsed into a spiritual coma. Such was the state of the church in Ephesus when Jesus addressed it with a rebuke. "Remember therefore from where you have fallen, and repent and do the first works . . ." (Rev. 2:5).

(9) The weekly communion supper on the Lord's day is one of the great institutions of Christianity. The design of this rite, at least in part, is to stimulate memory. Jesus said: "This do in remembrance of me" (Lk. 22:19). What a tragedy it is that so many neglect this sacred memorial for the most trivial of reasons (e.g., weekend recreational activities, family outings, etc.).

(10) How comforting it is to know that "God is not unrighteous to forget [our] work and the love [we] show toward his name" (Heb. 6:10). We may be assured that the Lord will keep all His promises to us.

Both "remembering" and "forgetting" are valuable abilities. But we must learn to distinguish between them. Remembering the wrong things, and forgetting the right ones, can be dangerous indeed. Let us thank the Creator for our amazing minds, and attempt to use them wisely to His everlasting glory.

Questions

1. How can a study of the "mind" of man be classified as "science"?

2. What is the significance of the statement that man is made in the "image" of God?

3. Discuss the difference between animal "instinct" and human "thinking."

4. Comment on Robert Jastrow's comparison of the human brain to the mechanical computer.

5. Discuss Loren Eiseley's description of how the human intellect got "jump-started."

6. Cite several examples of amazing memory feats.

7. Cite some examples of subconscious data that are "stored" in the brain.

8. Describe some of the emotional benefits of being able to "file" memories in the "back room" of the mind.

9. How can God be described as "remembering" and "forgetting"?

10. How can "remembering" the gracious acts of God be a motivation for godly living?

References

Asimov, Isaac (1970), *Smithsonian Institute Journal,* June.

Jastrow, Robert (1981), *The Enchanted Loom: Mind in the Universe* (New York: Simon & Schuster).

Miller, Benjamin & Goode, Ruth (1960), *Man And His Body* (New York: Simon & Schuster).

Pfeiffer, John (1961), *The Human Brain* (New York: Harper & Bros.).

Sagan, Carl (1979), *Broca's Brain* (New York: Random House).

Webster, Gary (1957), *Wonders of Man* (New York: Sheed & Ward).

CHAPTER 10

THE BIBLE AND MODERN PSYCHOLOGY

For the past several decades "psychology" has been a popular theme in American society. Countless students become "psychology majors" as they matriculate through school. The Yellow Pages of the phone book are filled with listings for psychologists and psychiatrists. For many, it is the "in" thing to have a therapist. Exactly what is "psychology," and how does this area of interest relate to the Bible?

Psychology Defined

Psychology may be defined in two very different ways — depending upon whether or not one is approaching the topic from the biblical vantage point, or from the humanistic viewpoint. The humanist, i.e., one who considers man to be the measure of all things, with no need for belief in a supreme Being, suggests that psychology is "the study of human and animal behavior." (We will probe this concept additionally later.) "Psychiatry," a related discipline, specializes in the diagnosis and treatment of psychological problems.

The term "psychology" actually derives from the Greek root, *psyche* (soul), and pertains, therefore, to a study of the soul (or spirit) of man.

One may affirm with confidence, that no "psychological" theory can benefit man that fails to consider the "soul" aspect. This would include such issues as: (a) Does the human being have a soul? (b) If so, where did it come from? (c) What is the nature of the human soul? (d) What is the purpose of man's soul? (e) Finally, what lies ahead as the ultimate destiny of the soul?

Man, the Soul Creature

In the balance of this chapter, we propose to highlight several glaring contrasts between biblical psychology and the psychology — falsely-called — that so dominates our modern culture.

There is a vast, unbridgeable chasm that exists between valid psychology and that which proceeds from a humanistic ideology. Let us probe some of the various questions just raised.

First, *does the human being possess a soul?* Logic demands, and the Bible affirms, that there is an entity within each human that sets him or her apart from all other biological creatures. This entity is the *soul*. One atheist, Julian Huxley, has even authored a book titled, *The Uniqueness of Man,* in which he acknowledged that, since the days of Darwin, when mankind was viewed strictly in animalistic terms, the "man-animal gap" has been "broadening" (Huxley, 3). By that he meant that it is becoming increasingly difficult to view human beings as mere animals. Another writer says that ". . . the very fact of human personality carries metaphysical overtones. Man's psychological nature suggests something transcendent of which the psyche is but a partial reflection" (Progoff, 256).

British poet-philosopher Samuel Taylor Coleridge wrote:

> "Either we have an immortal soul, or we have not. If we have not, we are beasts; the first and wisest of beasts it may be; but still beasts. We only differ in degree and not in kind; just as the elephant differs from the slug. But by the concession of the materialists we are not the same kind as beasts; and this also we say from our own consciousness . . . . it must be the possession of the soul that makes the difference" (Mead, 416-17).

Second, if we have a soul, *what is its nature?* Those who accept the Scriptures as the Word of God are bound to acknowledge that human beings possess an inward essence (cf. 2 Cor. 4:16) known as the "soul." Initially, let us observe that the term "soul" is found in at least three senses in scripture.

"Soul" is sometimes employed as a synecdoche (the part for the whole) to designate the entire person. Eight "souls" were saved in Noah's ark (1 Pet. 3:20). Every "soul" should submit to the civil authorities (Rom. 13:1), when such are not demanding a compromise of Christian principles (cf. Acts 5:29).

Additionally, the "soul" can denote biological life. In the Old Testament, all living creatures are said to possess "soul" (Gen. 1:30. *Nephesh* is the Hebrew term; the Greek equivalent is *psyche*, LXX). During a dangerous shipwreck en route to Rome, Paul informed his sailing mates that though the vessel would be destroyed, there would be no loss of "life" (*psyche*). He was referring to their physical lives.

Finally, and most significantly, is the use of *psyche* to designate that part of the human being that is in the very "image" of God (Gen. 1:26). In this instance *psyche* is the same as "the spirit" (*pneuma*). To this component of mankind various qualities are attributed. Consider, for example, the following:

(a) The "soul" cannot be destroyed by the termination of physical life. "And do not fear them that kill the body, but are not able to kill the soul . . ." (Mt. 10:28). Similarly, the "spirit" is said to be characterized by an "incorruptible" nature (1 Pet. 3:4).

(b) The *psyche* is capable of possessing knowledge. David declared: "I will give thanks unto you; for I am fearfully and wonderfully made: Wonderful are your works; and that *my soul knows* right well" (Psa. 139:14). In the New Testament, Paul rhetorically asks: "For who among men *knows* the things of a man, except the *spirit* of the man, which is in him" (1 Cor. 2:11).

(c) The *psyche* is an entity of emotion. In one of his defenses, the suffering Job argued that "[his] *soul grieved* for the needy" (30:25). Similarly, the prophet Daniel declared: *"My spirit was grieved* in the midst of my body" (7:15). As the Lord Jesus once contemplated the prospect of his impending death, he said: "Now is my *soul troubled*" (Jn. 12:27). Later, the apostle John would write: "[H]e was *troubled* in the *spirit* . . ." (13:21).

In modern humanistic "psychology," however, none of these matters is considered, and therein lies the worthlessness of the system. Humanism sees the universe as consisting exclusively of matter; *soul does not exist.* Can one be a true "psychologist" who does not even believe that human beings have souls? It is not without significance that the founders of modern psychology were men whose chief interests were in material or physical phenomena, e.g., chemistry, physics, and physiology (Cosgrove, 28).

Responsibility to the Creator

One of the underlying tenants of modern psychology is a skepticism about the existence of a supreme Being to whom man ultimately is accountable. Sigmund Freud (1856-1939), known as the founder of psychoanalysis, was a tremendously significant figure in the field of psychology. His influence permeated the educational field in many ways. Freud was an atheist who contended that religion is but an "illusion." He argued that early man did not understand the material forces of nature. Hence, out of that frustration, our ancestors felt "the need to make tolerable the helplessness of man." As a result, they "personified the forces of nature," and endowed them with qualities that reflected a "father-longing" (30,32,38).

Other dignitaries in the field also had atheistic inclinations. John Dewey (1859-1952), who exerted a vast influence over several disciplines (including psychology), and B.F. Skinner (1904-1990), a leading advocate of "behaviorism," both were signatories of the *Humanist Manifestos*, which utterly repudiated faith in God. Carl Rogers (1902-1987), prominent for the idea of "client-centered" therapy, was quite religious in his early years; eventually, though, he leased his brain to skepticism.

Here is a very important point. When men repudiate an awareness of the very Creator who designed them, they cannot possibly have a view of humankind that is normal and conducive to mental soundness. Humanistic psychology (which is the basis of virtually *all* modern psychology) is, therefore, bogus. And yet many, who profess a reverence for Christianity, are mesmerized by the theories of these men. One writer, for instance, in glowing language, says: "Carl Rogers seems to have brought a lot of God's truth to light by discovering some of God's principles for healthy human behavior" (Kirwan, 60). More on this later.

Evolutionary Presuppositions

As we mentioned earlier, modern psychology is generally defined as the study of "human and animal behavior." This very definition should be a "red flag" signal that we are talking about a school of thought that is grounded in evolutionary dogma. Dr. Paul W. Leithart has written: "All traditional psychiatry rests on two errors: 1) The acceptance of evolution; 2) Secular humanism" (8).

This point can be amply demonstrated; Charles H. Judd wrote: "If . . . psychology is to gain a complete understanding of human nature, it must take into account the findings of the science of biology, which traces man's bodily structures and some of his traits back to remote origins in the lower forms of animal life" (15).

One writer, in a book titled, *Apes, Men, and Language*, stated: "Darwin has provided the basis for a paradigm that might explain both human psychology and human behavior in terms of man's continuity with the rest of nature . . ." (Linden, 41).

After much research regarding this matter, Prof. Raymond Surburg concluded:

> "The evolutionistic influence on modern psychology must be traced back to Darwin's genetic approach to psychological problems or to his argument that man evolved from lower animal forms. It was his suggestion that many human expressions of emotion are merely continuations of actions useful in the animal, e.g., the sneer is a continuation of the animals' preparation to bite. A lengthy comparison of the mental powers of man and the lower animals was made by Darwin, who believed that animals showed evidence of imitation, curiosity, imagination, and even of reason. Darwin's genetic approach was extended to the study of animal, child, and racial psychology by a number of psychologists . . ." (184).

If modern humanistic psychology is grounded in Darwinism — and clearly it is — then the various theories that arise from this presupposition are as false as the doctrine of evolutionism itself.

Human Conduct

Psychological theory plays a significant role in either: 1) *explaining* man's conduct, or, 2) in *recommending* human activity. And herein lies one of the dangers. Reflect for a moment on these two points.

First, Sigmund Freud, and those who were influenced by him, argued that the "sex drive" is the primary force of all emotional life. This suggests that man is but a biological machine driven by the sex urge, which implies that such a dominating "instinct" leaves little (if any) room in man for the exercise of will and the expression of moral choices. This is why, more and more, we are hearing the refrain that human beings are not at fault *personally* for their aberrant conduct. We simply can't help what we do, it is alleged. For a further consideration of this point, see my book, *The Bible & Mental Health* (89-96).

Second, modern psychology not only attempts to rationalize man's behavior with mechanistic premises, frequently, it actually *encourages* wrong activities.

Earlier we mentioned the name of Carl Rogers. Rogers was a leader in the "humanistic revolution" in psychology. He became popular for his "client-centered" approach to therapy. Observe the following quotation, and how radically at variance it is with biblical morality.

> "It has seemed clear . . . that when the counselor perceives and accepts the client as he is, when he lays aside all evaluation and enters into the perceptional frame of reference of the client, he frees the client to explore his life and experience anew, frees him to perceive in that experience new meanings and new goals. But is the therapist willing to give the client full freedom as to outcomes? Is he genuinely willing for the client to organize and direct his life? Is he willing for him to choose goals that are social or antisocial, moral or immoral? If not, it seems doubtful that therapy will be a profound experience for the client . . . . To me it appears that only as the therapist is completely willing that *any* outcome, *any* direction, may be chosen — only then does he realize the vital strength of the capacity and potentiality of the individual for constructive action" (48-49).

Anyone remotely cognizant with New Testament ethics can perceive how destructive the Rogerian method is.

A Summary

As we conclude this brief survey of humanistic psychology, surely it has become evident to every reader who regards the Bible as a divine revelation, that there is a vast difference between modern, humanistic "psychology," and the wholesome mental health principles that abound in the Bible. Think about some of the vivid contrasts.

(1) Humanistic psychology alleges that the personhood of man can be explained solely in terms of a materialistic substance. But both the Bible and common sense affirm that there is more to man than matter. His self-awareness, conscience, emotions, ability to reason, aesthetic sensitivity, etc., all argue that "humanness" is far more than mere molecules in motion.

(2) Modern psychology asserts that human conduct is the result of impersonal forces (environment) that have acted upon our species over eons of time. We are the products of time and chance. Ultimately, therefore, there is no such thing as "good" or "evil." Traditional psychology is committed to "utter neutrality" in matters of morality (Liebman, 180-81). The *Humanist Manifestos I, II* asserts: "Ethics is *autonomous* and *situational*, needing no theological or ideological sanction" (17). This means that man is subject to no higher moral law than what he himself determines. Were that the case, there could

never be a "situation" during which one could do wrong! That is precisely the position argued by atheist Jean Paul Sartre. He contended that whatever one *chooses* to do is right; value is attached to the choice itself so that ". . . we can never choose evil" (279). By way of vivid contrast, the Bible teaches that human conduct is the result of the exercise of man's free will, and that bad choices, i.e., a violation of the law of God, as made known in the objective revelation of sacred Scripture, have resulted in the numerous problems that afflict the human race today. "God made man upright; but they have sought out many devices" (Eccl. 7:29).

(3) Traditional psychology contends that man's religious inclination (which, incidentally, is universal) is merely the result of an ignorant personification of the inexplicable forces of nature, endowing them with the "father" symbolism. But, the Bible teaches that there is a *real* Heavenly Father (Mt. 6:9), who genuinely cares for the human family, and who desires to rescue it from the consequences of its rebellion (Jn. 3:16).

(4) Modern psychology declares that since man is an evolved animal, the key to understanding his personality is to be discovered in studying animal behavior. In opposition, the Bible affirms that mankind is separate entirely from the animal kingdom, and only humans possess personhood.

(5) Secular psychology suggests there is no objective source of information to define the nature of human difficulties, and to address the remedy for these problems. The answers to mental ills, it is said, lie *within* the person. But, the Bible contends that the way of man is *not within*

himself; it is not in man to direct his own steps (Jer. 10:23). Moreover, the objective source of remedy is the divine revelation of Scripture (1 Cor. 2:6ff), amply documented by a wide variety of evidences. These inspired documents are able to satisfy completely every genuine need of the human mind (2 Tim. 3:16-17).

Conclusion

The fact of the matter is this: the reputation of humanistic psychology/psychiatry these days is somewhere between that of the alchemist and the snake-oil salesman. Sometime back, TIME magazine carried a major article titled: "Psychiatry's Depression." Dr. E.F. Torrey, a psychiatrist, has written a book dubbed: *The Death of Psychiatry.* Thomas Szasz, Professor of Psychiatry at the State University of New York, authored the shocking volume: *The Myth of Mental Illness* (1960), and O. Hobart Mowrer, an atheist who served as President of the American Psychological Association, produced a work called: *The Crisis in Psychology and Religion* (1962) in which he challenged the entire field of psychiatry for its dependence upon Freudian premises (see Adams, xvi).

The more one reflects upon the presuppositions of modern, humanistic psychology, the more he is inclined to think that Lucy, of the Charlie Brown comic strip, was overcharging when she gave counseling sessions for five cents!

Questions

1. How does modern humanism define "psychology"?

2. What is the real definition of "psychology"?

3. List some points which logically argue for the existence of a unique "soul" in human beings.

4. Name three ways in which the term "soul" is used in the Bible.

5. How did Sigmund Freud explain the origin of religion?

6. Can there be any true "psychology" without an acknowledgment of God? Explain.

7. Discuss Carl Rogers' "client-center" theory of psychology. What is the fallacy in this viewpoint?

8. To what principle is modern psychology committed in terms of moral conduct?

9. How is the following sentence contradictory: "Ethics is autonomous and situational."?

10. Why does modern psychology advocate the study of animal behavior?

References

Adams, Jay (1970), *Competent to Counsel* (Phillipsburg, NJ: Presbyterian & Reformed).

Cosgrove, Mark (1979), *Psychology Gone Awry* (Grand Rapids: Zondervan).

Freud, Sigmund (1949), *The Future Of An Illusion* (New York: Liveright Publishing).

Humanist Manifestos I & II (Buffalo, NY: Prometheus Press, 1973).

Huxley, Julian (1941), *The Uniqueness of Man* (London: Chatto & Windus).

Jackson, Wayne (1998), *The Bible & Mental Health* (Stockton, CA: Courier Publications).

Judd, Charles H. (1939), *Educational Psychology* (New York: Houghton Mifflin Co.).

Kirwan, William T. (1984), *Biblical Concepts for Christian Counseling* (Grand Rapids: Baker).

Liebman, Joshua (1946), *Peace of Mind* (New York: Simon & Schuster).

Leithart, Paul W. (1980), "Psychiatry and the Bible," *The Christian News*, September 15.

Linden, Eugene (1974), *Apes, Men, and Language* (New York: Penguin).

Mead, Frank (1965), *The Encyclopedia of Religious Quotations* (Westwood, NJ: Fleming Revell).

Progoff, Ira (1956), *The Death and Rebirth of Psychology* (New York: Julian Press).

Rogers, C.R. (1951), *Client-centered therapy* (Boston: Houghton-Mifflin).

Sartre, Jean Paul (1966), "Existentialism," reprinted in *A Casebook on Existentialism*, William V. Spanos, Ed. (New York: Thomas Y. Crowell).

Surburg, Raymond (1959), "The Influence of Darwinism," in *Darwin, Evolution, and Creation*, Paul Zimmerman, Ed. (St. Louis: Concordia).

CHAPTER 11

ARE SCIENCE AND FAITH COMPATIBLE?

Can one believe in the concept of a universe that was created by God, and still be respected in the modern world of "science"? Many people have been led to believe that faith in God, and the facts of science, are mutually exclusive propositions. As was mentioned in an earlier chapter, in one of his books, Vance Packard declared that "the discoveries of astronomers, geologists, and space explorers have undermined the faith of all but the most devout . . . ." He asserted that most of those who still believe in God probably see Him as some sort of "force," rather than a Person who is observing human behavior (p. 27). Has the god of *Star Wars* replaced the God of the Bible in the minds of many?

Some writers suggest that the advent of Darwin's evolution theory made it no longer necessary to believe in God. In the book, *The Blind Watchmaker,* which argues for "a universe without design," Richard Dawkins asserts that "Darwin made it possible to be an intellectually fulfilled atheist" (6). Steve Allen, the comic whose varied entertainment skills have given him a platform for the advocacy of his skeptical ideas, contends that "the inability to believe in God as traditionally defined has indeed become increasingly common in the intellectual and scientific community during the past two centuries" (328). These quotations are typical of those whose "god" has become pseudo-science.

The historical reality is this: atheism did not bring us the age of science. A recent writer concedes: "It is widely accepted on all sides that, far from undermining it, science is deeply indebted to Christianity and has been so from at least the scientific revolution. Recent historical research has uncovered many unexpected links between scientific enterprise and Biblical theology" (Russell, 777). Professor J. Macmurray, certainly no friend to Christianity, confessed: "Science is the legitimate child of a great religious movement, and its genealogy goes back to Jesus." Similarly, Nikolai Berdyaev, a Marxist philosopher who taught at Moscow University, declared: "I am convinced that Christianity alone made possible both positive science and technics" (Smethurst, 21).

Atheists, to some extent, have attempted to hijack the domain of science within the past hundred years or so; but in reality, some of the greatest scientific leaders of history have been religious people. Many of them were driven to explore the mysteries of the creation because they were intrigued with the genius of Him whom they acknowledged as the Architect of the universe. Not a few of these luminaries were serious students of the Bible and revered it as the Word of God. Let us reflect upon some of these dignitaries who have bequeathed a rich legacy to our modern era.

Johann Kepler (1571-1630)

Johann Kepler was "one of the greatest astronomers that ever lived" (Wright, Vol. 13, 398). Though he made numerous discoveries (e.g., the tides are caused by the moon), he is most famous for three astronomical laws which he recognized. First, he noted that the planets travel around the sun in an elliptical orbit, with the sun at one focus of the ellipse. Second, he found that a planet's speed increases as it nears the sun, but decreases as it gets farther away; but no matter what its speed may be, a line drawn between it and the sun will always sweep over exactly the same area of space in the same length of time. Third, the time a planet takes to circle the sun depends on its distance from the sun. The square of the time it takes will be exactly in proportion to the cube of its average distance away. Kepler's discoveries prepared the way for the work of Isaac Newton.

As Kepler studied the heavens, he was awed by the power and wisdom of God. He once said that in his discoveries he was merely "thinking God's thoughts after Him." He wrote: "I thank Thee, my Creator and Lord, that Thou hast given me this joy in Thy creation, this delight in the works of Thy hands; I have shown the excellency of Thy works unto man, so far as my mind was able to comprehend Thine infinity" (Northrop, 266).

Blaise Pascal (1623-1662)

A very remarkable French mathematician and philosopher was Blaise Pascal. Pascal had taught himself geometry by the time he was twelve years of age. At sixteen, he had completed a book on the subject. He was the first to set forth what is called the theory of probability. Pascal is best recognized, however, for his discovery that liquid in a vessel carries equal pressure in all directions. This is known as Pascal's Law. The principle is used in hydraulic jacks, vacuum pumps, air compressors, etc. This brilliant man of science also invented a calculating machine.

As fascinated with science as he was, Pascal was even more intrigued with religion. He certainly did not subscribe to the notion that faith and science are incompatible. In fact, Pascal maintained that "the only perfect knowledge [comes] through Christian revelation" (Jones, 167). His famous book, *Pensees,* which reflected his thoughts on religion, was subtitled, *An Apology for the Christian Religion.* "Apology" means a defense.

Robert Boyle (1627-1691)

The "father of modern chemistry" was Robert Boyle. Boyle experimented with the expansion and compression of air and other gases. This led to the formulation of an important law in physics (known as Boyle's Law), which suggests that in a gas at constant temperature the volume is inversely proportional to the pressure. This law has had tremendous significance for science and industry. Boyle was the first to suggest the idea of a chemical "element." He argued that atoms of one kind of matter make up all substances, and that the differences in substances are the result of the differing arrangements and movements of the atoms.

As Boyle matured, his interest in religion accelerated. He became convinced that the Bible is a divine revelation. He studied Hebrew and Greek in order to be able to read the Scriptures in their original languages. He contributed to the distribution of Bibles in several different languages. One biographer observed that his thinking became "more devout the more he studied the wonders of nature . . . . At his death Boyle left a sum of money to found the Boyle lectures . . . intended for the confutation of atheism" (Hall, 382).

Sir Isaac Newton (1642-1727)

Sir Isaac Newton has been called "one of the greatest names in the history of human thought" (Cohen, 306). Albert Einstein once paid tribute to Newton by suggesting that his own work would have been impossible but for the discoveries of Newton. At the age of twenty-seven he was known as an "unparalleled genius." Isaac Newton's achievements were remarkable in a number of areas. In mathematics, he invented the discipline known as calculus. He was the first to describe the concept of universal gravitation and to note that the planets are held in place by this force. Newton's discoveries in the area of optics were also phenomenal. By examining sunlight as it passed through a prism, he showed that white light is made up of the colors of the rainbow. He also invented the reflecting telescope.

In addition to his scientific contributions, Isaac Newton was a deeply religious man. He was as much a student of the Scriptures as he was science. He authored several theological works. As a result of his studies of the universe, Newton wrote: "This most beautiful system of the sun, planets, and comets, could only proceed from the counsel and dominion of an intelligent and powerful

Being" (Hutchins, 369). He was buried in Westminster Abby where a monument reads: "Let mortals congratulate themselves that so great an ornament of human nature has existed."

Michael Faraday (1791-1867)

Michael Faraday "is ranked as one of the most brilliant experimentalists science has ever known" (Sewell, 146). Each time you ride in an automobile or switch on your lights, you owe him a debt. He made the first electric motor, the first dynamo, and the first transformer. He discovered benzol, the basis of aniline dyes, and he was the first to detect the phenomenon known as polarization of light, which established a connection between light and electricity. For more than a half century he did astounding work in the fields of chemistry and electricity at the Royal Institution in London; he authored 158 scientific papers, listed in the catalogue of the Royal Society.

Faraday's religious convictions were widely known. An agnostic associate said of him: "I think that a good deal of Faraday's week-day strength and persistency might be referred to his Sunday Exercises. He drinks from a fount on Sunday which refreshes his soul for a week." A biographer notes that Faraday's sense of the "unity of the universe derived from the unity and benevolence of its Creator" was the motivating factor in his scientific drive. He devoutly believed that God was the maker and sustainer of all things (Williams, 527). Another writer notes: "Like Pasteur, Faraday was inspired in his scientific work by his simple but steadfast belief in the will of God" (Wright, Vol. 13, 385).

Louis Pasteur (1822-1895)

The father of modern bacteriology was Louis Pasteur. His contributions to medicine, chemistry, and industry were profound indeed. Pasteur "was the first to show that living things come only from living things" (Dubos, 170). This, of course, is the basis of the scientific Law of Biogenesis (life comes only from life), and it disproved the evolutionary concept of spontaneous generation — which argues that somehow life must have come from non-life originally. Pasteur, who is acknowledged even by atheism as "one of the greatest scientists in history," was a strong opponent of Darwin's theory of evolution by natural selection (Asimov, 425). This renowned scientist discovered that the sterilization of food substances will kill the microbes. The process, known today as "pasteurization" (coined from his name), has saved countless lives. This great man also discovered that diseases are caused by germs that invade the body. He found that if one's body is inoculated with a weakened form of the microbe, it will produce an immunity. The process of vaccination resulted from his work. Pasteur's accomplishments in industry were many. He saved the silk industry by isolating a germ that was destroying silkworms, he combated fowl cholera and anthrax in cattle, and developed the treatment for rabies. These are but a sampling of his astounding achievements.

Rather than destroying his belief in God, Pasteur's

brilliant discoveries made him humble as he contemplated the marvels of divine creation. He argued that the notion of "spontaneous generation (like materialism in general) threaten[s] the very concept of God the Creator" (Geison, 371).

George Washington Carver (1864-1943)

In a discussion of scientists who sought to honor God by their endeavors, it is a difficult task to decide which ones to include for consideration. George Washington Carver is selected because his unusual accomplishments took their rise from such a humble background. Carver was born to slave parents whom he never knew. At the age of ten, he set out on his own to educate himself, which he did, finally receiving a master's degree in 1896. He became the director of agricultural research at Tuskegee Institute in Alabama the same year. From scrap-heap odds and ends, Carver constructed a laboratory, out of which came some truly amazing developments. For example, Dr. Carver (his only doctorate was honorary) developed 118 different products from the sweet potato (e.g., tapioca, starch, vinegar, molasses, library paste, rubber, etc.). From pecans he produced more than 60 different items, and some 300 synthetic products from the peanut, including milk, cheese, coffee, ink, dye (30 kinds), shoe polish, cereal, soap, wood stain, insulation board, etc. Carver once invited some friends to dinner. He served salad, soup, a creamed vegetable, "chicken," coffee, cookies, and ice cream. What his guests didn't know was that he made all of these items from peanuts!

George Washington Carver marvelled at God's fascinating creation. He arose daily at 4:00 a.m. for solitary walks in the woods. He told a friend, "At no other time have I so sharp an understanding of what God means to do with me." Every Sunday at Tuskegee he conducted an afternoon Bible class, during which he read the Scriptures and talked of God and nature.

Dr. Carver was once asked why he developed such an interest in the peanut. Tongue-in-cheek, he told this story. One day, while talking with God, he asked: "Mr. Creator, why was the universe made?" He said the Lord told him: "You want to know too much. Your mind is too small to know that." "Well," he inquired, "why then did you make man?" To which the Creator responded: "Little man, you still want to know too much." Finally, he asked: "Well, Mr. Creator, what's the peanut for?" And the Lord said: "That's more like it!" Carver said his work on the peanut was an attempt to discover why God made it (Moore, 88). Carver received numerous tributes, both in America and abroad. He would never have entertained the notion that science and religion are mutually exclusive.

Wernher von Braun (1912-1977)

One of the pioneers of modern rocketry was Wernher von Braun. Dr. von Braun was perhaps the leading force behind America's space program. His team developed the four-stage Jupiter rocket that launched Explorer I, the first United States satellite. Another of his projects was the launching of the Saturn V rocket which put the first astronauts on the moon. Von Braun was considered one of the world's foremost rocket engineers.

Dr. von Braun recognized that science alone can never satisfy the soul. He wrote: "It is as difficult for me to understand a scientist who does not acknowledge the presence of a superior rationality behind the existence of the universe as it is to comprehend a theologian who would deny the advance of science. Far from being independent or opposing forces, science and religion are sisters . . . . There is certainly no scientific reason why God cannot retain the same position in our modern world that He held before we began probing His creation with the telescope and cyclotron" (Von Braun, 35, 38).

Conclusion

Quack religionists and pseudoscientists (and some are an admixture of both) may be antagonists, but genuine religion and true science are not. The fact is, many scientists are giving serious consideration to religion in these times of technological stress. Science writer Lincoln Barnett, in his book, *The Universe and Dr. Einstein*, commented that the continuing discoveries of modern science have made it "more difficult" to ignore the idea of God (22). James Jauncy, who holds ten academic degrees, authored a significant volume titled, *Science Returns To God*. Therein he wrote: "The atheist or the hostile agnostic, even in scientific circles, is becoming a rare bird indeed" (17).

Agnostic science writer, Robert Jastrow, probably

said more than he intended when he concluded one of his books in the following fashion: "For the scientist who has lived by his faith in the power of reason, the story ends like a bad dream. He has scaled the mountains of ignorance; he is about to conquer the highest peak; as he pulls himself over the final rock, he is greeted by a band of theologians who have been sitting there for centuries" (Jastrow, 116).

God has gloriously revealed Himself — in nature, and in His holy book, the Bible. Explore His message, and honor Him in your life each day.

Questions

1. Why do many people today feel that faith in a personal God is rather obsolete?

2. How did Richard Dawkins assess the influence of Charles Darwin?

3. Have some reputable scholars conceded that science has benefited from the influence of Christianity? Cite a reference.

4. What was a chief motivation behind the explorations of many of the pioneers of science?

5. How did Johann Kepler's observations of the order of the universe mold his religious ideas?

6. What was the sub-title of Pascal's famous book, *Pensees*?

7. Cite Isaac Newton's testimony regarding the origin of the ordered universe.

8. What science principle did Louis Pasteur discover that is so devastating to the theory of organic evolution?

9. What motive did George Washington Carver site as that which stimulated him to explore the lowly peanut?

10. Though Robert Jastrow is an agnostic, what did he confess as

he concluded his book, *God and the Astronomers?*

References

Allen, Steve (1993), *More Steve Allen on the Bible, Religion, & Morality* (Buffalo, NY: Prometheus Books).

Asimov, Isaac (1982), *Asimov's Biographical Encyclopedia of Science and Technology* (New York: Doubleday & Co.).

Barnett, Lincoln (1959), *The Universe and Dr. Einstein* (New York: Mentor).

Cohen, I. Bernard (1979), *The World Book Encyclopedia* (Chicago: Worldbook-Childcraft International, Inc.), Vol. 14.

Dawkins, Richard (1986), *The Blind Watchmaker* (New York: W.W. Norton & Co.).

Dubos, Rene (1979), *The World Book Encyclopedia* (Chicago: Worldbook-Childcraft International, Inc.), Vol. 15.

Geison, Gerald L. (1970), *Dictionary of Scientific Biography*, Charles C. Gillispie, Ed. (New York: Charles Scribner's Sons), Vol. X.

Hall, Maria Boas (1970), *Dictionary of Scientific Biography*, Charles C. Gillispie, Ed. (New York: Charles Scribner's Sons), Vol. II.

Hutchins, Robert M., Ed. (1952), *Great Books of the Western World* (Chicago: Encyclopedia Britannica), Vol. 34. Sir Isaac Newton's *Mathematical Principles of Natural Philosophy* — 1687.

Jastrow, Robert (1978), *God and the Astronomers* (New York: W.W. Norton & Co.).

Jauncey, James (1971), *Science Returns to God* (Grand Rapids: Zondervan).

Jones, Phillip S. (1979), *The World Book Encyclopedia* (Chicago: Worldbook-Childcraft International, Inc.) Vol. 15.

Moore, Eva (1971), *The Story of George Washington Carver* (New York: Scholastic Book Services).

Northrop, Stephen Abbot (n.d.), *A Cloud of Witnesses* (Cincinnati: John F. McCurdy).

Packard, Vance (1968), *The Sexual Wilderness* (New York: David McKay Co.).

Russell, Colin (1984), *Nature* 308, April 26.

Sewell, W. Stuart (1949), *Brief Biographies of Famous Men and Women* (New York: Permabooks).

Smethurst, Arthur F. (1955), *Modern Science and Christian Beliefs* (New York: Abingdon Press).

Von Braun, Wernher (1981), "Science Verifies God," *Science and Religion,* David L. Bender & Bruno Leone, Eds. (St. Paul: Greenhaven Press).

Williams, L. Pearce, *Dictionary of Scientific Biography,* Charles C. Gillispie, Ed. (New York: Charles Scribner's Sons), Vol. IV.

Wright, Ernest & Mary (1962*), Richards Topical Encyclopedia* (New York: The Richards Co., Inc.).

CHAPTER 12

THE BIBLE AND ARCHAEOLOGY

In the 18th year of his administration (c. 621 B.C.), Josiah, king of Judah, was having repairs done on the ancient Jewish temple in Jerusalem. During the task a most important discovery was made. A copy of the "book of the law" was found in the ruins. When this text of God's word was shown to be in glaring contrast with the practices of the day, the young king initiated a reform that had an important, if only temporary, effect (2 Chron. 34:14ff). Though this was not a formal archaeological "find;" nonetheless, it reveals how a discovery from the past can impact the future.

As a science, "archaeology" is still relatively young — about two centuries old. But thrilling discoveries have been made that continue to draw attention to the sacred writings, collectively known as the Bible.

"Archaeology" derives from *archaeios* (ancient), and *logos* (study); hence, this discipline is a "study of the ancient." This science involves the investigation of ancient sites, buildings, tools, and other objects, as a way of learning about man's history.

The Past Considered; the Process Pursued

Ancient civilization is a story of decay and destruction. Cities were destroyed by invading armies. New communities were built upon the ruins of the old, until, in many cases, several levels of occupation were layered, one on top of the other. The archaeologist probes down through these strata looking for treasures of antiquity.

In making these explorations, a variety of scientific studies may be a part of the process. The zoologist could be needed to identify bones, the botanist will study the remains of seeds or plants to determine food sources or clothing fibers, while the mineralogist may be sought for metal analysis. Language experts will be needed, of course, to decipher ancient texts. It really is a rather complicated process.

The Vast Range of Evidence

A number of dramatic archaeological discoveries have been made since the early 1800's. More than half a million cuneiform (tiny, wedge-shaped letters) clay tablets have been found in the region extending to the east of the Mediterranean Sea. Hundreds of inscriptions have been discovered in Asia Minor and Europe. Papyri (ancient "paper" made from the papyrus plant) manuscripts have been uncovered in Palestine and in Egypt. The amount of material has been staggering — and there is more to come. It is estimated that of the 5,000 possible sites for excavation in Palestine alone, less than 200 have been explored. Of the several hundred thousand clay tablets that lie collecting dust in museum basements, only about 10% have yet been translated (Yamauchi, 155).

The importance of archaeological study has been manifold. (1) This science has aided us in locating many biblical locations that were once lost in the obscurity of antiquity. (2) Archaeological study has thrown a flood-light on the customs of the biblical world, thus illuminating many scripture texts. (3) The meanings of many of the biblical words have been clarified by their use in ancient documents. (4) Archaeological investigation has helped with establishing biblical chronology, and the relationship of the Scriptures to secular history. (5) Archaeology has enhanced our confidence in the accuracy of the biblical records, supporting their claims of divine inspiration. The charges of the critics have been increasingly silenced.

Some Important Discoveries

We have space in this brief chapter for only a few references to some of the remarkable discoveries that have been made during the past two centuries.

(1) In 1843, French explorer Paul Botta discovered Khorsabad (in Assyria). The palace of Sargon II, the conqueror of Samaria and destroyer of the kingdom of Israel, was uncovered. When fully excavated, the ruins of the palace compound covered an area of 25 acres. Two years later, Henry Layard, an English archaeologist, uncovered Nineveh. Its walls were 32 feet thick and 76 feet high. The remains of Ashurbanipal's library were found. He was the grandson of Sennacherib, who is mentioned in the Old Testament (2 Kgs. 18; Isa. 36). This depository of data contained fragments of some 26,000 clay tablets, including historic, scientific, and religious literature (Pfeiffer, 101).

(2) Between 1925 and 1931, some 20,000 tablets

were exhumed in northern Iraq (at Nuzi). These Babylonian documents provided information about the culture in 15th-14th centuries B.C. They greatly support the historicity of the patriarchal period in Genesis, as D.J. Wiseman of the University of London has shown (Douglas, 69).

(3) At Mari, in southeast Syria, some 20,000 clay tablets were discovered between 1933 and 1960. They date to the 18th century B.C., and are in a Semitic dialect that is "virtually identical" to that spoken by the Hebrew patriarchs.

(4) Beginning in 1947, in the region just west of the Dead Sea, some 500 documents, collectively known as the Dead Sea Scrolls, were found. They contain both biblical and non-biblical writings. About 100 of the scrolls are Old Testament books, written in Hebrew. At least portions of all Old Testament books (except Esther) were found. This was one of the most significant archaeological discoveries ever made. This discovery, which pushed our knowledge of the Old Testament text back about 1,000 years earlier than copies previously possessed, established how very accurately the sacred Scriptures had been transmitted across the centuries.

(5) Since 1929 there have been intermittent excavations at Ras Shamra (on the Syrian coast opposite Cyprus). Several hundred texts were uncovered which shed an amazing amount of light on the Canaanite religion in the 15th-14th centuries before Christ. A study of these texts has demonstrated that the earlier liberal claims, that Israel's religion was borrowed from the Canaanites, was utterly false. One scholar says that the

Ras Shamra evidence reveals that Canaanite mythology and Israelite theology "are as far apart as east and west" (Kelso, 1444).

For a more extensive discussion of these, and other fascinating discoveries, see our book, *Biblical Studies in the Light of Archaeology*. Let us now give consideration to some of the contributions that the science of archaeology has made to the study of the Holy Scriptures.

Chronology

One of the benefits of archaeological study has been the correlation of Bible events with secular history, thus establishing the historical context of certain biblical records. One example from the New Testament relates to Paul's labor in Corinth. According to Luke's record, the Jews in Corinth rose up against Paul and brought him before Gallio's judgment seat (Acts 18:12). Near the commencement of this century, in the city of Delphi (on the northern side of the Gulf of Corinth, six miles inland), a mutilated inscription was discovered that mentions Gallio (with his official title, "proconsul"), and dates the time of his administration. Based upon this information, and that in Acts, scholars argue with fairly strong confidence that the apostle arrived in Corinth in about December of A.D. 49 (Finegan, 282).

Obscure Passages

For years Bible students were puzzled about the meaning of some obscure passages in the divine Book.

Sometimes they had to simply guess at the meanings, since there was no parallel information to illuminate the enigmatic texts. Happily, though, archaeological enlightenment has been of some assistance.

At the age of 120 years, it was said of Moses that "his eye was not dim, nor his natural force abated" (Dt. 34:7). But what does the expression "natural force" mean? Since the Hebrew term was similar to a word for "jaw," some (e.g., Jerome) assumed the prophet's teeth was the focus of the passage. In the Ras Shamra tablets, though, the word was twice used of manly vigor (Free, 62).

The point is this: Moses' death was due to his disobedience in the wilderness, and not because he was a worn-out old man who just could not go on. The passage stresses the importance of being obedient to Jehovah.

Historical Accuracy

If the Bible is the inspired word of God, one has every right to expect it to be accurate in its historical information. Down through the years, though, unfriendly critics have been quick and sharp in criticizing the sacred narrative. It has been alleged on numerous occasions that the Bible is characterized by historical blunders. The patient work of the archaeologist, however, has evaporated these charges like mist in the morning sun. Several of these examples of "mistakes" will now be cited.

(1) While the patriarch Abraham sojourned in Egypt, he was given "camels" by the ruling Pharaoh (Gen. 12:16). Camels are also mentioned as some of the

victims of one of the plagues visited upon the Egyptians during the days of Moses. Liberals once classified these references as "obvious error." As a consequence of archaeological studies, it is now known that the camel was present in Egypt as early as 3,000 B.C. — centuries before the time of Abraham, as Professor Kenneth Kitchen has clearly shown (Douglas, 182).

(2) The first mention of "writing" in the Bible is in Exodus 17:14. Numerous other references follow this one. Again, hostile critics charged that no alphabetic script existed in the days of Moses — in spite of the fact that Jesus referred to Moses' "writings" (Jn. 5:46-47). T.K. Cheyne contended that the Tora (law) was not written until 1,000 years *after* Moses (II.2055). No one would dream of making that statement today. The fact is, samples of a Proto-Semitic alphabet have been found in the Sinaitic Peninsula that date back centuries before Moses (see Finegan, 126).

(3) For some time, skeptics have questioned the historicity of David, Israel's greatest king. A writer in *The Anchor Bible Dictionary* says that "many scholars are skeptical about the possibility of ever recovering a true picture of the 'historical' David" (in: Freedman, 2:48). But astounding archaeological data, confirming the biblical narrative, have come to light in recent years. David's name, on an inscription dating to the 9th century B.C., has been found near the city of Dan (close to the source of the Jordan River). Dr. Bryant Wood calls this "one of the most important discoveries in the annals of Biblical archaeology" (121).

(4) Isaiah tells of Sargon, king of Assyria, sending

his forces against Ashdod (a Philistine city in SW Palestine) (Isa. 20:1). Prior to the year 1843, Sargon's name was not found in any piece of ancient literature — save Isaiah's record. And so, in typical fashion, Isaiah was charged with an historical error. In the aforementioned year, however, P.E. Botta discovered Sargon's palace about a dozen miles north of Nineveh. The prophet Isaiah was thus fully vindicated.

(5) Liberal critics of the Bible have frequently alleged that Acts is not a reliable document from the standpoint of history. F.C. Baur (1792-1860) of Germany popularized this view more than a century ago. This notion, however, has been thoroughly discredited.

Sir William Ramsay (1851-1939), a British scholar, initially questioned the historicity of Acts, but after years of literally digging up the evidence in archaeological explorations, Ramsay became convinced that Acts was so remarkably accurate in its details, that the whole of it must be considered trustworthy.

In one of his famous books, he honestly admitted his earlier skepticism:

> "I had read a good deal of modern criticism about the book, and dutifully accepted the current opinion that it was written during the second half of the second century by an author who wished to influence the minds of people in his own time by a highly wrought and imaginative description of the early Church. His object was not to present a trustworthy picture of facts in the period about A.D. 50, but to produce a certain effect on his own time by setting forth a carefully coloured account of events and persons of that older period. He wrote for his contemporaries, not for truth" (37-38).

After much investigation, though, Ramsay continued:

> "The present writer takes the view that Luke's history is unsurpassed in respect of its trustworthiness. At this point we are describing what reasons and arguments changed the mind of one who began under the impression that the history was written long after the events and that it was untrustworthy as a whole" (81).

J.B. Lightfoot (1828-1889) was one of the greatest scholars of his day. Fluent in seven languages, he made vast contributions to the literature of the New Testament. In one of his works defending the supernatural character of the New Testament, he said of the book of Acts: ". . . [N]o ancient work affords so many tests of veracity; for no other has such numerous points of contact in all directions with contemporary history, politics, and topography, whether Jewish, Greek, or Roman" (19-20).

In more recent times, Henry J. Cadbury, the liberal scholar of Harvard University, authored a volume titled, *The Book of Acts In History*, in which he introduced many examples of the amazing accuracy of Luke's second letter to Theophilus.

Luke records an abundance of details, and this allows the careful student to check the ancient historian for credibility. For instance, the physician-historian mentions thirty-two countries, fifty-four cities, and nine Mediterranean islands. In addition, he alludes to ninety-five different people, sixty-two of which are not mentioned by any other New Testament writer. Twenty-seven of these are unbelievers, chiefly civil or military officials (Metzger,

171-172). The book of Acts will definitely stand the test of historical examination.

The Integrity of the Biblical Text

Do we really know that the text of our English Bible is essentially that of the original Hebrew and Greek manuscripts? Yes indeed. Again, the science of archaeology has been a willing witness for the integrity of the biblical text.

Robert Dick Wilson was a renowned Bible scholar who taught at Princeton University. A master linguist (familiar with 45 languages), Professor Wilson spent 15 years carefully examining the Hebrew text of the Old Testament, comparing it with inscriptions taken from the ancient monuments (e.g., the names of rulers, etc.). He published the cream of his research in a book titled, *A Scientific Investigation of the Old Testament.* Here is what he concluded: ". . . [I]t is my endeavor to show from the evidence of manuscripts, versions, and the inscriptions, that we are scientifically certain that we have substantially the same text that was in the possession of Christ and the apostles and, so far as anybody knows, the same as that written by the original composers of the Old Testament documents" (8).

The same sort of compelling evidence exists for the New Testament as well. There are more than 5,000 Greek manuscripts (in part or in whole) of the New Testament text. Some of these extend to the very shadows of the first century. There are some 10,000 ancient translations from the Greek into other languages; some of these reach back to the 2nd and 3rd centuries A.D. Then there are hundreds of quotations from the New Testament in the writings of the Greek and Latin fathers. It has been said that the text of the New Testament could be reproduced almost entirely from these writings alone.

In fact, it has been shown that there is much greater credibility for the New Testament — though it has been in existence for nineteen centuries — than there is for the writings of William Shakespeare — produced just four centuries ago (Hastings, 13)!

Conclusion

We are thankful indeed for the work of skilled archaeologists over the years. Though many of them today are far from being conscientious Bible believers, they have, nonetheless unwittingly assisted in enhancing our understanding of, and confidence in, the Holy Scriptures as the inspired word of God.

Truly, dead men have told tales!

Questions

1. Define "archaeology," and discuss what the goal of this branch of science is.

2. List several different scientific disciplines that may be needed as companions in the examination of archaeological data.

3. Discuss the range of evidence that has been explored thus far, and compare it with what is yet to be done.

4. List five values of pursuing the study of biblical archaeology.

5. Rehearse the findings at both Khorsabad and Nineveh. What is the significance of Nineveh in biblical history?

6. State a major importance of the Dead Sea scrolls find.

7. What is the importance of understanding the significance of Moses' health (Dt. 34:7) at the time of his death?

8. How did early critical claims — that writing was unknown in the time of Moses — reflect upon the integrity of Christ?

9. Discuss the significance of Botta's discovery of Sargon's palace.

10. What caused Sir William Ramsay to alter his views of Luke's credibility as an historian?

11. Cite some instances of Luke's careful details in the book of Acts.

12. Discuss the range of evidence for the integrity of the New Testament text.

References

Cheyne, T.K. (1899), *Encyclopedia Biblica* (London: A.&C. Black).

Douglas, J.D. , Ed. (1974), *The New Bible Dictionary*, (Grand Rapids: Eerdmans).

Finegan, Jack (1946), *Light from the Ancient Past*, (Princeton: Princeton University).

Free, Jack (1999 - Revised*), Wycliffe Dictionary of Theology* E.F. Harrison, G.W. Bromiley, C.F. Henry, Eds. (Peabody, MA: Hendrickson).

Freedman, David N., Ed. (1992*), The Anchor Bible Dictionary* (New York: Doubleday).

Hastings, H.L. (1881), "Corruptions of the New Testament," *A Square Talk to Young Men About the Inspiration of the Bible* (Elgin, IL: Brethren).

Kelso, James (1998), *Wycliffe Bible Dictionary*, C.F. Pfeiffer, Howard Vos, John Rea, Eds., (Peabody, MA: Hendrickson).

Lightfoot, J.B. (1889), *Essays of the Work Entitled Supernatural Religion* (London: MacMillan).

Metzger, Bruce (1965), *The New Testament: its background, growth, and content* (New York: Abingdon).

Pfeiffer, Charles F., Ed. (2000), *The Wycliffe Dictionary of Archaeology* (Peabody, MA: Hendrickson).

Ramsay, William (1979), *The Bearing of Recent Discovery on the Trustworthi-*

ness of the New Testament (Grand Rapids: Baker).

Wilson, Robert Dick (1929*), A Scientific Investigation of the Old Testament* (New York: Harper Bros.).

Wood, Bryant G. (1993), *Bible and Spade*, Vol. 6, No. 4.

Yamauchi, Edwin (1972*), The Stones and the Scriptures* (Philadelphia: Holman).

CHAPTER 13

THE BIBLE, GEOGRAPHY, AND ANCIENT CULTURE

Is the Bible really a credible book? Did it derive from the times, and out of the ancient settings, that it claims? Does it have the "ring" of authenticity? Can we trust it as a spiritual guide?

There are two kinds of information in the Scriptures — that which is checkable and that which is not. For example, there is no way to verify scientifically the existence of the human "soul." Some have sought to weigh a terminally ill patient — before and after death — to determine the weight of the soul. Such efforts are futile, for the non-material is not subject to scientific experimentation. When one submits to the apostolic command to be baptized for the remission of sins (Acts 2:38; 22:16), it is useless to analyze the baptismal water subsequent to the rite in order to determine the nature of the penitent's sins. Forgiveness takes place in the mind of God, not literally in the water.

Here is the point: if one is able to verify the Scriptures in matters that are checkable, and they prove to be *infallibly accurate in every detail*, then it is perfectly reasonable to conclude that the balance of the Bible is just as accurate. No *strictly human* document — of the same size and age as the Bible — can pass this test of inerrancy; but the Bible does. It is possible, therefore, to have a firm confidence that the Scriptures are reliable in issues that are not subject to objective demonstration. That is why it is important to challenge the sacred writings, in a respectful way, to determine whether or not they bear the marks of integrity.

In 1858, a remarkable volume was authored by W.M. Thomson, a long-time missionary in Syria and Palestine. The composition, titled *The Land and the Book*, was written to show the marvelous harmony between the text of the divine Scriptures, and the ancient land out of which they largely came. The author contended that there are a "thousand witnesses to the veracity of the Bible which meet the pilgrim at every turn in his pathway" (Author's Preface).

J.W. McGarvey was once characterized by the *London Times* as the ripest Bible scholar on either side of the Atlantic. In 1879, after having taught Sacred History at the College of the Bible (Lexington, Kentucky), McGarvey left his old Kentucky home and journeyed to the Bible lands to further complement his knowledge of the sacred Scriptures. He studied in Egypt, Palestine, Syria, Asia Minor, and Greece. The result of his labor was a highly acclaimed volume of more than 600 pages, called *Lands of the Bible* (1880).

McGarvey presented an ingenious case for the divine character of the Bible, based upon hundreds of incidental references to geography, customs, and culture that are found on its pages. The vein of his argument was this: a fictitious narrative, located in a country with which the writer is not personally familiar, must either avoid local allusions, or frequently be found in conflict with peculiarities of place, customs, etc. (375).

McGarvey therefore carefully compared the biblical text with the actual facts relating to "the land." He acknowledged that the validity of his conclusions would depend upon: (a) the number of points of agreement between the Bible and the facts of the case relative to the land; (b) the minuteness of the concord; (c) the uncontrived way in which the material is presented; (d) a complete absence of disagreement between the respective bodies of information (384).

His confident conclusion, with reference to the Bible's agreement with the facts related to Palestine, finally was this:

> "Its plains, mountains, valleys, rivers, lakes, cities, and deserts are in all parts of the Bible correctly named and correctly located. The political divisions known to exist are invariably recognized, as are also all the changes of government through which the country passed in the course of its long and varied history. *In not a single known instance, is there a failure in any one of these particulars*" (377, emp. WJ)

This eminent scholar then observed that the Scriptures are unique in this respect. No writer, ancient (e.g., Josephus) or modern (e.g., Rollin), is so perfectly precise as the sacred record.

With deep gratitude to both Thomson and McGarvey, we introduce the following data.

Topography
Even though the biblical writers did not possess the sophisticated instruments of measurement that we have

at our disposal today, they flawlessly allude to elevational circumstances. A casual survey of a Bible concordance will reveal that there are hundreds of references to travel wherein a party will be said to "go up" or "go down" to a particular place. Contrary to our casual custom of describing our visits "up north" or "down south," the Scriptures' "ups" and "downs" are always literal. Folks travel from Judea "down" to Antioch, even though the latter is to the north of the former (Acts 15:1-2). When one travels from Jerusalem "down" to Jericho (Lk. 10:30), he may be certain that there is an elevation drop — in this case 3,200 feet in the seventeen-mile distance!

Compass Points

A good test of a writer's knowledge of a region is how well he is able to describe the relative locations of various places. It is very easy to get our "easts" and "wests" confused, and our "norths" and "souths" turned around. The Bible writers never do. When Lot left "uncle" Abram at Bethel, and made his way toward the well-watered region near Sodom, he was traveling "east" (Gen. 13:11), but when Daniel foretold the conquests of Alexander the Great, symbolically depicted as a powerful "he-goat," he depicted the warrior's assaults as originating from the "west" (Greece) (Dan. 8: 4). When Jeremiah alluded to Babylon's threat to Judah, the ominous force is described as peering down from the "north" (6:1). But why, a critic asks, does the Bible allude to Abraham going "South," when he was leaving Egypt, journeying to Canaan (Gen. 13:1), when Canaan is *north* of Egypt? Because "South"

(Heb. *negeb*) is a technical term for the region that covers southern Palestine-northern Sinai. This is not a mistake; it is another example of technical accuracy!

Flora and Fauna

It is always a test of a writer's skill to examine whether his allusions to plants and animals of a certain locale are correct or not. The Bible comes through with flying colors.

There have been no lions in Palestine for at least seven centuries, and there may have been few, if any, during the days of Christ, since there is no mention of them in either the Gospel Accounts or in Acts. But, according to the Scriptures, they prowled the region in Old Testament times (the Hebrew Old Testament even has seven different words for the lion). David had an encounter with the "king of beasts" (1 Sam. 17:34). But the biblical record has been shown to be accurate. A large basalt monument has been found at Beth-shan (a city where the valleys of Jezreel and Jordan meet), showing a dog and a lion in combat (Stern, I.216). It dates to the mid-2nd millennium B.C.

Jeremiah, in contrasting the keen instincts of certain Palestinian migratory birds, with dull Israel, wrote: "The stork in the heaven knows her appointed times; and the turtledove, and the swallow and the crane observe the time of their coming, but my people know not the judgment of Jehovah" (8:7). In the authoritative work on Bible animals, Cansdale notes that Palestine is a major corridor for migratory birds (150-160).

Frequent mention is made in the Old Testament of "oak" trees, and today, there are 24 species of the oak in Palestine. Generally, though, it is too warm in the valleys of Canaan for these trees; they mostly thrive in the mountain areas. It was in the mountain region east of the Jordan that Absalom was caught by his hair as he rode a mule beneath an oak tree (2 Sam. 18:9). Thomson notes that this locale was "celebrated for [its] great oaks" (243). Moreover, in most countries it would be quite difficult to get caught in the "thick" boughs of an oak tree, as the branches are generally too high or too sparse to accommodate such a tragedy, but the Palestinian environment is in perfect agreement with the narrative. (McGarvey, 379).

Most people assume that fruit trees produce but one crop each year. With figs, however, it is different. They produce two crops annually (sometimes three). Tiny figs appear in March, but most fall off the tree (cf. Rev. 6:13). Then, there are the "first ripe figs" (of June — Isa. 28:4). Finally, there are those that mature in August (possibly alluded to as the "summer" fruit mentioned in Amos 8:1-2). In our land, a tree may be fully leafed while the fruit is still small, but in first-century Palestine when a fig tree was completely leafed, it indicated that fruit was normally present. When Jesus found the odd fig tree that had leaves, but *no fruit,* He skillfully used it as an object lesson to predict the destruction of the *fruitless* Jewish nation (Mk. 11:13-14). McGarvey observed that the figs grown in Palestine when he visited there "are formed *after* the leaves come out" (McGarvey, 58; emp. WJ). Again, the Book is true to the ancient land.

Customs

The practices of particular societies vary from place-to-place and from time-to-time. It is, therefore, a good test of an author's credibility to note how meticulous he is in describing the manners and customs of the people about whom he writes. If he incorporates data that are obsolete, he is suspect. On the other hand, if a writer has the minutest of incidentals absolutely correct, one may indeed conclude that this is strong evidence of the integrity of the record. How do the biblical documents measure up to this standard? Quite well. Some examples will prove helpful.

(1) How is the modern student to explain Jesus' statement: "Give, and it shall be given you: good measure, pressed down, shaken together, and running over, shall men give into your bosom" (Lk. 6:38). What in the world does "into your bosom" mean? Such an expression makes little sense to the current resident of New York City. But the language is perfectly understandable within the context of first-century society. In that day the common working person wore a long, coarse robe that reached virtually to the ground. It could be bound around the waist with a "belt" or a sash. When one bound his sash tightly, the merchant could pour grain into the top of the robe. The garment literally became a sack. The Lord thus was teaching that generosity pays; when one generously gives to others, God will see to it that his "sack" is overflowing! The passage bears the mark of *antiquity.*

(2) In the period of the patriarchs, neither paper money nor coinage were used as media of exchange. Orig-

inally, folks simply bartered (traded) their goods. The Hebrew word for "purchase" is *miqnah,* and it is kindred to *miqne,* "cattle." The verb came to simply mean "buy," regardless of the form of exchange (cf. Gen. 17:12), but the term has the ring of authenticity based upon this early method of commerce. When men first begin to use precious metals for purchasing objects, they was measured by "weight." Abraham paid for the field of Machpelah by "weighing out" silver (Gen. 23:16). Archaeologists have uncovered many ancient "weights" by which silver and gold were measured. According to the ancient historian Herodotus (1.94), the Lydians were the first people to issue coins. The New Testament writers employed some seven different terms for various denominations of coinage of that era. And the descriptives are all absolutely true to factual history.

(3) Cedar from the forests of Lebanon was used for many objects during the Old Testament era — such as ships (Ezek. 27:5), idols (Isa. 44:14), and buildings (2 Sam. 5:11). But in first-century Palestine, wood was not employed in houses. They were constructed of sun-dried bricks or stone; wood was rarely used, even for rafters and joists. Large slabs of stone were employed instead. It was these houses of dried brick to which the Lord referred when he spoke of thieves "breaking through" and stealing one's treasure (Mt. 6:19). The Greek literally means "to dig through" (see ASVfn). Houses were built wall-to-wall and were flat-topped. The house-top was thus a convenient place for private meditation. To suggest in our day that a preacher was on the housetop praying (cf. Acts 10:9), might invoke a rather bizarre

image! Moreover, Jesus' admonition that when the assault against Jerusalem (by the Romans) commenced, the faithful were not to go down from the housetop (Mt. 24:17), makes perfect sense when one recognizes that these hard-joined dwellings constituted what was known as the "road of the roofs" (Edersheim, 94), which would accommodate rapid escape from the doomed city. The Bible is true to its historical periods.

(4) Ancient Palestine was known for its very fine grapes. When the Israelite spies returned from their reconnaissance of Canaan, they brought a sampling of grapes so large that two men bore one cluster on a staff between them (Num. 13:23). The valley where the grapes were retrieved was named Eshcol ("cluster"). This area just north of Hebron is known for its grapes to this day. At this time, the Israelites were familiar only with Egyptian grapes, which are very small.

But there are examples of huge grapes in the Mediterranean region. One writer sites the case of a cluster that weighed 45 pounds, and Clarke mentions that he himself had cut a cluster that weighed nearly 20 pounds (I.661). There is mention in the Bible of winepresses that were "hewed" or "dug" (Isa. 5:2; Mt. 21:13). McGarvey notes that these winepresses "were used only by ancient Jewish inhabitants of the country" and they have not been in use for the past 2,000 years (381). But remnants of these winepresses are seen even today, a photo of one being found in *The Zondervan Pictorial Encyclopedia of the Bible* (Tenney, 5.937).

Conclusion

The Bible critic is certain to dismiss these interesting "little" bits of information as insignificant. And perhaps they would remain rather unnoticed as isolated pieces of data. Yet, in concert, they form a pattern of technical precision that is uncanny. These are not the sort of facts that are contrived. They are incidental, and they are tell-tale signs of authenticity. They are compelling evidences of the great truth that the Bible is indeed what it claims to be — the inspired word of God.

Study it carefully, believe it implicitly, yield to it wholeheartedly, and embrace its promises happily.

Questions

1. What two categories of information are found in the Bible? How does one relate to the other?

2. Describe McGarvey's method of ascertaining the integrity of the Bible based upon geography, customs, etc.?

3. After a careful study of these areas of Bible information, what was professor McGarvey's conclusion?

4. Give an example of a correct elevation allusion in the Scriptures. Also cite a reference involving a compass point?

5. How could the Bible be accurate in referring to Canaan as the "South" in its relationship to Egypt?

6. Cite some examples of how the Bible may be tested in terms of its animals and plants.

7. How does a knowledge of fig trees in Palestine help to clarify Jesus' actions in Mark 11:13-14?

8. What did the Lord mean by the expression, "they shall give into your bosom" (Lk. 6:38)?

9. How does Christ's warning about thieves "breaking through"

one's house conform to the construction practices of the first century?

10. Is Moses' reference to the size of grapes in Canaan credible? Explain.

References

Cansdale, George (1970), *All the Animals of the Bible Lands* (Grand Rapids: Zondervan).

Clarke, Adam (n.d.), *Commentary on the Holy Bible* (Nashville: Abingdon).

Edersheim, Alfred (1957), *Sketches of Jewish Social Life In the Days of Christ* (Grand Rapids: Eerdmans).

McGarvey, J.W. (1881), *Lands of the Bible* (Philadelphia: J.B. Lippincott).

Stern, Ephraim, Ed. (1993), *The New Encyclopedia of Archaeological Excavations in the Holy Land* (New York: Simon & Schuster).

Tenney, Merrill, Ed. (1975), *The Zondervan Pictorial Encyclopedia of the Bible* (Grand Rapids: Zondervan), Five Volumes.

Thomson, W.M. (1863), *The Land and the Book* (London: T. Nelson & Sons).